PIVOT TABLES

AF785055

TABLE OF CONTENTS

Legal Notes and Disclaimer

Text Copyright © Andrei Besedin.

All rights reserved. No part of this guide may be reproduced in any form without permission in writing from the publisher except in the case of brief quotations embodied in critical articles or reviews.

Legal & Disclaimer

The information contained in this book and its contents is not designed to replace or take the place of any form of medical or professional advice; and is not meant to replace the need for independent medical, financial, legal or other professional advice or services, as may be required. The content and information in this book has been provided for educational and entertainment purposes only.

The content and information contained in this book has been compiled from sources deemed reliable, and it is accurate to the best of the Author's knowledge, information and belief. However, the Author cannot guarantee its accuracy and validity and cannot be held liable for any errors and/or omissions. Furthermore, changes can be periodically made to this book as and when needed. Where appropriate and/or necessary, you must consult a professionalbefore using any of the suggested remedies, techniques, or information in this book.

Upon using the contents and information contained in this book, you agree to hold harmless the Author from and against any damages, costs, and expenses, including any legal fees potentially resulting from the application of any of the information provided by this book. This disclaimer applies to any loss, damages or injury caused by the use and application, whether directly or indirectly, of any advice or information presented, whether for breach of contract, tort, negligence, personal injury, criminal intent, or under any other cause of action.

You agree to accept all risks of using the information presented inside this book.

You agree that by continuing to read this book, where appropriate and/or necessary, you shall consult a professional before using any of the suggested remedies, techniques, or information in this book.

FEATURE # 01 USING LISTS FORMATTED TABLE AS DATA SOURCE

Out of many useful features of Pivot Tables, one of the most desirable features is its ability to use List formatted as Table working as its data source. These Lists provide a means to store data in a *more* useful format that can be readily used by Pivot Tables unlike conventional Excel Tables (that are not formatted as table).

Below is outlined a procedure for creating List for Pivot Tables:

FORMATTING LIST FOR PIVOT TABLES:

Create a Header Row:

We need a header row in the top most row of a table or list. Usually it is formatted a little different from rest of the data and for the ease of use. We should use "Freeze Pan" with this header row to make scrolling easier.

> To insert freeze pan, select the row just below where you want to freeze pan, point to *Tab View> Freeze Pan> Freeze Pan* to make row stay at the top while you scroll.

Append Data:

Once done with header row, you can append data below it. Append it serial wise or date wise so that validation is easier – this way you can cross check if the data for a particular day or date or ID.

Format as Table:

Even it is ok to use lists for pivot tables, but you can *convert* them to Tables. The tables are great because with tables, you don't need to update the range reference every time. Point the pivot table only once to the data and keep appending below it, the pivot table will be updated automatically.

S	T	U
Product Containe	Product Base Margir	Ship Date
Small Box	0.36	5/15/2010
Jumbo Drum	0.4	5/17/2010
Small Box	0.59	4/20/2011
Small Box	0.38	9/14/2012
Small Box	0.54	9/17/2009
Jumbo Drum	0.66	10/10/2010
Small Box	0.38	7/16/2012
Jumbo Drum	0.58	7/31/2011
Jumbo Box	0.65	8/9/2010
Small Box	0.38	8/11/2010
Small Pack	0.41	4/10/2011
Small Box	0.56	4/9/2011
Medium Box	0.65	2/11/2009

This blue box represents a table...

- You can convert a *normal table* into *excel table* by pressing Ctrl+T.
- You will see a *blue square* at the right bottom corner of the table once it has been *turned* into a MS Excel Table.

Advantages of Using List in Pivot Table:

Using List as Database

You can use the list as database in Excel. The data can be appended under the header row and even if it consists of hundreds of rows. Thus you don't need to worry about where you will be storing data, it can simply reside by side of a Pivot in an Excel worksheet.

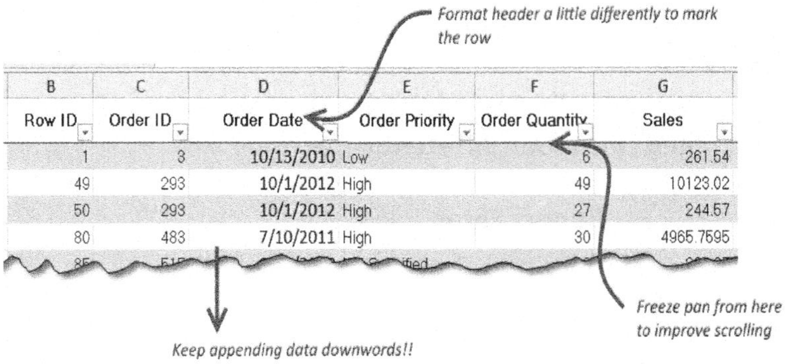

Updating is Pivots is Easier with Lists:

Yes, using *lists* makes it easier to update the Pivot Table. One just needs to press the refresh button and there you go! The Pivot Table is updated! Thus with lists, you can put names of all the required fields in the top row and append the data on daily basis, just below what has been put there earlier.

CONCLUSION:

You can turn our raw data into a formal excel table very quickly and after that there will be no need to manually update the ranges in the pivot table –that will improve the performance of our pivot table.

Feature # 02 Creating Scenarios with Filters

One of the Excel's Pivot Table ability that is of great use for analyzing data is that it allows for drilling down the data in many ways. This is one of the most prominent advantages of using a pivot table over simple Data Tables.

As we create pivot tables, we will be asked to arrange filed[1] into four different categories:

Report Filter
Column Labels
Row Labels
Values

Parts of a Pivot Table:

A Report Filter:

A report filter is used to add fields that we want to use as filter for the entire Pivot Table. It means that when we filter out data from here, the rest of the pivot table will be adjust with respect to all the three parameters (Column, Row label and Values) and gives an updated result.

Column Label:

A Column Labelis used to put the variable we want to see in the top most row of the Pivot Table.

Row Label:

The Row Labelis used to put the variable we want to see in the left most column of the pivot table.

Values:

In this area we put the variable we want to analyze.

CREATING THE PIVOT TABLE:

This is done by selecting the data and going to **TabData>Insert Pivot Table** and pressing Ok.

Place the field that you want to create scenarios for in the **Report Filter** Section. This will allow you to filter that field and that filter will change the entire Pivot Table. You can select multiple criteria for filtering from here.

- You can add multiple criteria's or fields to this filter – this is in addition to the selection of multiple criteria's within each field.

- In order to select multiple criteria's at once, you need to check mark the option "Select Multiple Options" from the same criteria selection menu.

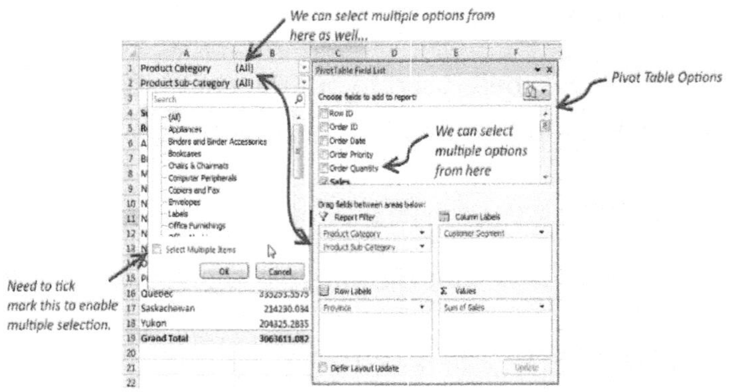

Once the Pivot Table is successfully inserted, we have to add fields to different sections of the pivot table (Row and Column Labels). Here the user needs to decide what will be the layout of the Pivot Table.

In Value we need to put the variable you want to get results for.

Once we are through step # 4, we are actually done by setting up the pivot table. You can now drill down the data with your filters on the top and using filter on the row and column labels.

Using Row and Column Label filters to modify the report:

Just like Report Filters, the Column, and Row filters are there to help you select show what is required. In order to reach these filter:

Select the row/column Label dropdown.

You will be able to see the options that can be selected or unselected.

Select / unselect or do multiple selections by pressing ctrl keys.

- If you are comfortable with using keyboard for navigation, you can use Alt + Down key to enable dropdown filter of Pivot table.

EXAMPLE OF ANSWERING QUESTIONS WITH FILTERS:

Referring to the data in the sample sheet – we can answer question based on the data set. For example we might be interested in finding:

Breakup of various segments over provinces for different categories and subcategories.

Determining shipping cost for various provinces and various shipping modes for given priority level.

Let's take these examples one by one and see how filtering pivots can answer these questions:

Breakup of various segments over provinces for different categories and subcategories.

Here we have five factors that we need to take into account:

Customer Segments

Provinces

Categories
Subcategories
Sales

We will be using these fields to see how the data is behaving. In order to produce a Pivot Table that does so, we need to arrange the fields in the following manner:

Put categories into the Report filter.
Also place subcategories just below categories in the report filter as well.
Place segments on the row label section.
Place Provinces in the column label section.
Put sales in the values area.

The resulting arrangement is shown in the following picture.

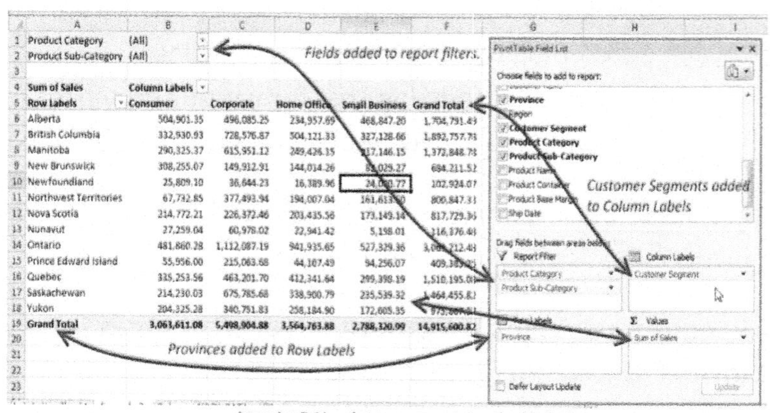

Arranging field so that we we can analyse the distribution of sales....

From the report, it is clear that corporate sector is the biggest customer segment drawing highest sales for the firm. This is followed by Home office and Consumer. When it comes to analyzing sales over provinces, it is can be seen that Ontario has highest sales volume, followed by Alberta. The lowest sale is found to be at Newfoundland.

Determining shipping cost for various provinces and various shipping modes for given order priority

This is the second example where we want to see how shipping cost varies for different provinces and the various shipping modes that are being used by the company when we have different *"levels of priority"* or *"urgency"* in common terms. We are actually interested in finding the *"Total costofshipping for each case"*. For this scenario to build up and explained we have to setup a pivot table:

For this pivot table, following variables or factors are to be taken into account:

Provinces
Shipping Cost
Shipping Mode
Level of Priority

We arrange these filed in the following manner to get the desired pivot table:

Put Provinces to the row label in pivot table.
Place Shipping cost to the value field.
Put Shipping mode it he column label.

Place Level or Priority in the Report Filter area.

Arranging this way will result in a pivot table that looks like in the following picture.

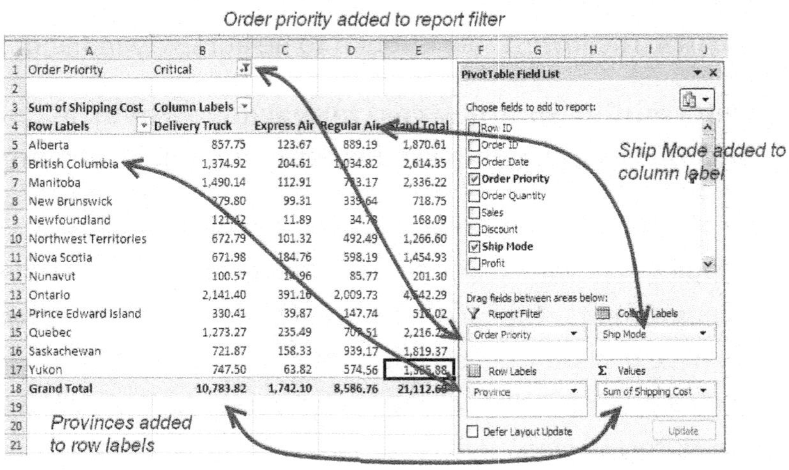

Arranging fields to analyze the distribution of Shipping Cost....

Analysis of the table reveals that the biggest contributor to the shipping cost is Ontario followed by British Columbia. Similarly the most concentrated mode of shipping is Delivery Trucks with the second one in the series is Regular Air. Further that if we drill down further to this table, we will find that Ontario the Delivery truck and Regular air are two major modes of transportation.

The table can still be drilled down. We can select option from the level of priority from the report filter to see how cost varies with the level of priority or urgency. For example for shipments marked *"critical"* the shipment mode used most frequently is Delivery Trucks – one might expect it to be express air but figures does not support it, followed by *"Regular air"* mode. A similar behavior is found when we see data for shipments with *"low"* level of urgency, the Delivery Truck and Regular air takes the biggest chuck.

CONCLUSION:

In this way, we can arrange fields and filter them to get insights into the data. The ease of use of arranging variables or fields in the pivot is reasons why it is used so frequently in practical life.

FEATURE # 03 FILTERING OPTIONS FOR ROW AND COLUMN LABELS

So far, we have added fields to the Pivot Table and used single or multiple report filters for drilling down data and producing meaningful analysis. Yet another very powerful feature of pivot table is that it allows user to filter for the row and column label as well.

This means that after selecting a particular scenario, you can look for a certain criteria or set of criteria to 16further improve your analysis.

- The feature is very beneficial for larger pivot tables, where it is difficult to focus on a small set of criteria.
- Filtering a pivot table is also beneficial when it comes to printing pivots on paper. It is very important that all the needed information is there in that single paper sheet.

EXAMPLE OF FILTERING ROWS AND COLUMN LABELS

Let's take up another scenario where we are interested in following question:

"How the company's sales are distributed over "Customer Segments" and "Product Categories" and "Product Sub Categories"?

We need to arrange a pivot table with following variables:

Product Categories and Sub Categories
Customer Segments
Sales
Order Date (Optional)

And they are to be added in the following areas of pivot table:

Place Product Categories and Sub Categories in the Row Label – place Sub category just below the Product Categories.
Sales in the value field.
Customer Segments in the column label.
Order Date in the Report Filter area – but it is optional, it can also be skipped.

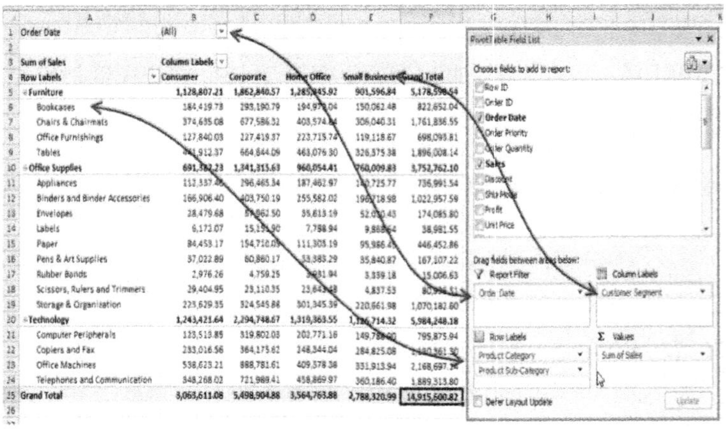

PROCEDURE FOR FILTERING:

Point your cursor to the Row or Column Label Dropdown.

As you will click, you will be displayed options available for filtering.

Select the options you want to display.

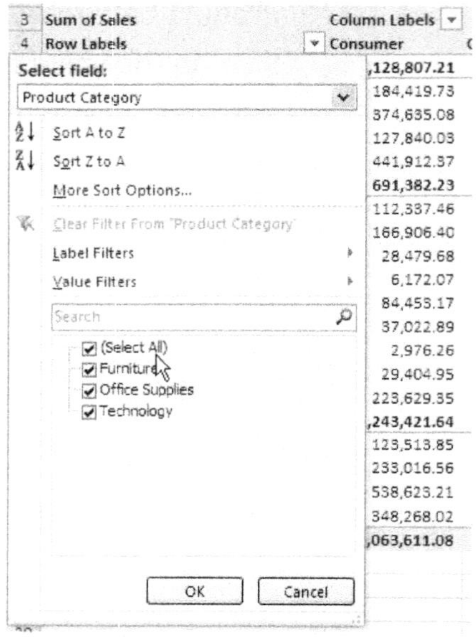

Besides selecting from the menu to display variables, we can filter row labels for various other options as well:

You can use Label Filters: This allows user to filter Label texts for text criteria. This is helpful when you have several Row labels with similar texts, you can filter out of them using Label Filter Option.

You can use Value filters: If you have values or numbers in row labels for example if you have dates as row labels, you can filter them using this option. You can filter data for values between two points, less then or grater then options.

CONCLUSION:

There are situation when don't want to display certain row or column label in the pivot table (for example blank entries). These two filtering options help make pivot table more professional.

Feature # 04 Levels of Summaries

As a data analyst, you must have used subtotals. Subtotals are great way to see the breakup of your data set. The same feature is available in pivot table to see details and to make summaries from the same table. The dock down feature of pivot table is added when you stack more than one field in the column or row label areas.

How to setup Levels in A Pivot Table:

Choose your required fields.
Add required number of fields to Report filter area and the values area
Add fields to row and column labels
Add more than one field to row and column label and even the value area
You should be able to see the level hierarchy on the left and the top side of the pivot table
Dock down details or undock as your requirement states.

- You can stack more than one variable over one another to get different degree of complexity in a pivot table.
- These levels can be docked or undocked depending on your requirement by pressing "+" and "-"symbol just in front of the level hierarchy.

AN EXAMPLE OF SETTING UP AND USING LEVELS IN PIVOT TABLE:

Let's take up question! A data analyst is interested in finding how the profit is spread over various product categories. In order to answer the question he sets up a pivot table that has:

Product Category added to row labels
Profit added to values section

... And the table looks like:

4	**Row Labels**	**Sum of Sales**
5	Furniture	5,178,590.54
6	Office Supplies	3,752,762.10
7	Technology	5,984,248.18
8	**Grand Total**	**14,915,600.82**

No Levels

You can see that level of details is minimal in this example. As one move further, he might be interested in finding how this profit is further divided into various subcategories. In order to view the breakup, simply stack Sub Category variable below Product Category variable

.... The result is shown in the following picture. You can see a small minus sign inside a box on the left side of the table this shows that details of the table. If you want to see the summary, simply click it and it will turn into a plus sign signaling that you may see further details if needed.

It might be required to know how different Regions do in terms of profit. The details are obtained by adding another field of Regions just above the Product Category field.

Row Labels	Sum of Sales	Sum of Profit
⊟Furniture	**5,178,590.54**	**117,432.99**
Bookcases	822,652.04	(33,582.13)
Chairs & Chairmats	1,761,836.55	149,649.73
Office Furnishings	698,093.81	100,427.92
Tables	1,896,008.14	(99,062.53)
⊟Office Supplies	**3,752,762.10**	**518,021.46**
Appliances	736,991.54	97,158.06
Binders and Binder Accessories	1,022,957.59	307,413.42
Envelopes	174,085.80	48,182.60
Labels	38,981.55	13,677.17
Paper	446,452.86	45,263.20
Pens & Art Supplies	167,107.22	7,564.78
Rubber Bands	15,006.63	(102.67)
Scissors, Rulers and Trimmers	80,996.31	(7,799.25)
Storage & Organization	1,070,182.60	6,664.15
⊟Technology	**5,984,248.18**	**886,313.52**
Computer Peripherals	795,875.94	94,287.48
Copiers and Fax	1,130,361.30	167,361.46
Office Machines	2,168,697.14	307,712.93
Telephones and Communication	1,889,313.80	316,951.64
Grand Total	**14,915,600.82**	**1,521,767.96**

Level of Details

Row Labels	Sum of Sales	Sum of Profit
⊟Atlantic	**2,014,248.20**	**238,960.61**
⊟Furniture	**708,726.78**	**15,345.65**
Bookcases	139,521.13	7,886.9
Chairs & Chairmats	197,849.60	13,177.7
Office Furnishings	100,429.00	6,575.9
Tables	270,927.05	(12,294.9
⊟Office Supplies	**478,464.42**	**66,970.4**
Appliances	145,403.14	24,516.97
Binders and Binder Accessories	120,696.97	36,529.02
Envelopes	17,227.92	4,256.41
Labels	5,234.23	2,138.41
Paper	67,140.87	11,075.05
Pens & Art Supplies	18,455.57	746.98
Rubber Bands	1,520.66	78.62
Scissors, Rulers and Trimmers	3,264.92	(792.18)
Storage & Organization	99,520.14	(11,578.83)
⊟Technology	**827,057.00**	**156,644.51**
Computer Peripherals	96,752.30	14,474.98
Copiers and Fax	171,963.09	12,885.32
Office Machines	306,322.74	88,127.06
Telephones and Communication	252,018.87	41,157.15

Three Level of details

Further details can be added to the Pivot Table - for example by adding variables to Column fields (for example customer segment) to see how all these variables break into different customer segments and then analysis can be done to produce something like below:

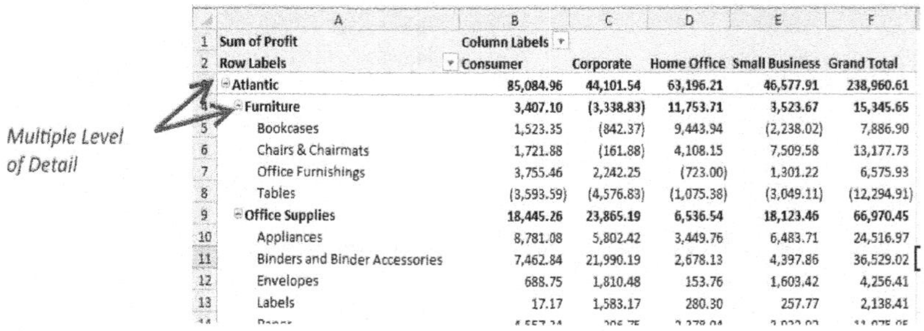

	A	B	C	D	E	F
1	**Sum of Profit**	**Column Labels**				
2	**Row Labels**	**Consumer**	**Corporate**	**Home Office**	**Small Business**	**Grand Total**
3	**Atlantic**	**85,084.96**	**44,101.54**	**63,196.21**	**46,577.91**	**238,960.61**
4	**Furniture**	**3,407.10**	**(3,338.83)**	**11,753.71**	**3,523.67**	**15,345.65**
5	Bookcases	1,523.35	(842.37)	9,443.94	(2,238.02)	7,886.90
6	Chairs & Chairmats	1,721.88	(161.88)	4,108.15	7,509.58	13,177.73
7	Office Furnishings	3,755.46	2,242.25	(723.00)	1,301.22	6,575.93
8	Tables	(3,593.59)	(4,576.83)	(1,075.38)	(3,049.11)	(12,294.91)
9	**Office Supplies**	**18,445.26**	**23,865.19**	**6,536.54**	**18,123.46**	**66,970.45**
10	Appliances	8,781.08	5,802.42	3,449.76	6,483.71	24,516.97
11	Binders and Binder Accessories	7,462.84	21,990.19	2,678.13	4,397.86	36,529.02
12	Envelopes	688.75	1,810.48	153.76	1,603.42	4,256.41
13	Labels	17.17	1,583.17	280.30	257.77	2,138.41

In the same way, you can add more than one field to the value field to see them side by in the following manner:

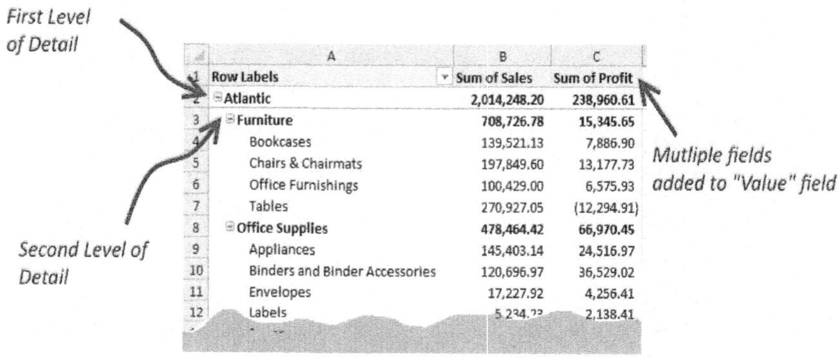

	A	B	C
1	**Row Labels**	**Sum of Sales**	**Sum of Profit**
2	**Atlantic**	**2,014,248.20**	**238,960.61**
3	**Furniture**	**708,726.78**	**15,345.65**
4	Bookcases	139,521.13	7,886.90
5	Chairs & Chairmats	197,849.60	13,177.73
6	Office Furnishings	100,429.00	6,575.93
7	Tables	270,927.05	(12,294.91)
8	**Office Supplies**	**478,464.42**	**66,970.45**
9	Appliances	145,403.14	24,516.97
10	Binders and Binder Accessories	120,696.97	36,529.02
11	Envelopes	17,227.92	4,256.41
12	Labels	[illegible]	2,138.41

CONCLUSION:

The pivot table allows you to add more than one to row and column labels and the value field. It gives us options to see different levels of details from the same pivot table.

FEATURE # 05 TOTALING OPTIONS IN A PIVOT TABLE

With pivot tables, we can manipulate variables to generate meaningful reports. These reports are meaningless, if the values are not totaled. But we don't need values to be summed always. We might require values to averaged, we might require it be variance or some other sought of analysis to be done.

With Pivot table totaling options, we summarize the values in the way that we want. Pivot table's values section is the area where we set all these options.

FUNCTIONS AVAILABLE FOR SUMMARIZING DATA:

If you click the dropdown menu of the pivot table, you will find following options available for summarizing variable you put in this section:

Sum
Count
Average
Max
Min
Product
Count Numbers
StdDev
StdDevp
Var
Varp

You can see that it is not only sum that is available to be used. We will take up couple of examples to see how to use them.

- There are about 11 function including SUM that can be used to summarize the data in the pivot table.

Taking up the Pivot Table that we first created the default values shows by it are the sum.

	A	B	C	D	E
1					
2	Product Category	(All)			
3					
4	**Sum of Order Quantity**	**Column Labels**			
5	**Row Labels**	**Delivery Truck**	**Express Air**	**Regular Air**	**Grand Total**
6	Consumer	5723	4733	31304	41760
7	Corporate	10682	9280	58555	78517
8	Home Office	6545	6347	39915	52807
9	Small Business	5814	4993	30886	41693
10	**Grand Total**	**28764**	**25353**	**160660**	**214777**

SUM is the default options

CALCULATING AVERAGE SALES FOR DIFFERENT CONSUMER TYPES:

Select any cell in the bottom row that shows total for the shipment mode variable.
Selecting this will enable the Pivot Table Tab in Excel's top section.
On the left top you can see the "Field Setting" Option.

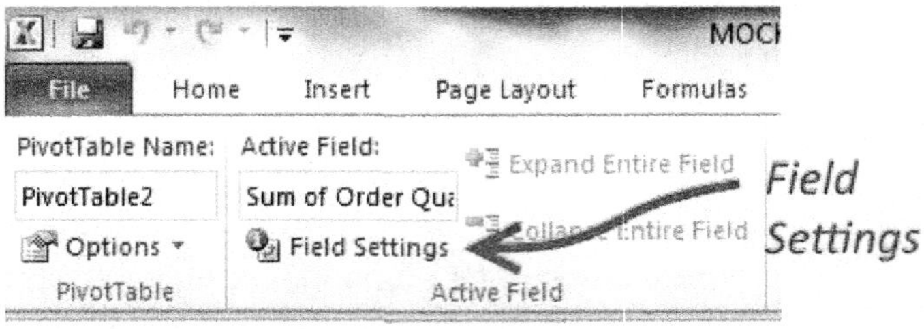

Click the option, it will show the following dialogue box.

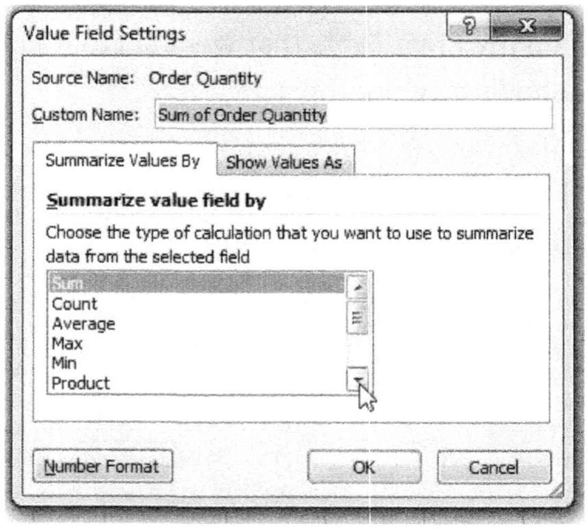

Select "Average" and press Ok.

The following figures will be shown in the resulting pivot table.

	A	B	C	D	E
1					
2	Product Category	(All)			
3					
4	**Average of Order Quantity**	**Column Labels**			
5	**Row Labels**	**Delivery Truck**	**Express Air**	**Regular Air**	**Grand Total**
6	Consumer	24.88	24.65	25.51	25.32
7	Corporate	25.37	25.64	25.54	25.53
8	Home Office	24.61	27.01	26.07	25.99
9	Small Business	25.39	25.74	25.34	25.39
10	**Grand Total**	**25.10**	**25.79**	**25.62**	**25.57**

Similarly if one had selected "Count", the result would have been:

2	Product Category	(All)			
3					
4	**Count of Order Quantity**	**Column Labels**			
5	**Row Labels**	**Delivery Truck**	**Express Air**	**Regular Air**	**Grand Total**
6	Consumer	230.00	192.00	1,227.00	1,649.00
7	Corporate	421.00	362.00	2,293.00	3,076.00
8	Home Office	266.00	235.00	1,531.00	2,032.00
9	Small Business	229.00	194.00	1,219.00	1,642.00
10	**Grand Total**	**1,146.00**	**983.00**	**6,270.00**	**8,399.00**

If you are interested in finding standard deviation of the order quantity for all product categories and for a given shipment mode you can set the value field setting to standard deviation. This will show following result.

2	Product Category	(All)			
3					
4	**StdDev of Order Quantity**	**Column Labels**			
5	**Row Labels**	**Delivery Truck**	**Express Air**	**Regular Air**	**Grand Total**
6	Consumer	14.84	13.86	14.21	14.25
7	Corporate	14.88	13.95	14.59	14.55
8	Home Office	14.19	14.21	14.67	14.56
9	Small Business	14.94	13.56	14.54	14.48
10	**Grand Total**	**14.71**	**13.92**	**14.52**	**14.48**

..Most of the orders have a standard deviation of approximately 15%. (100±15)

CONCLUSION:

There are multiple options available in pivot table to summarize the row total or column total. Out of this spectrum of option it is up to the user what to use.

Feature # 06 Relative Totaling Options in a Pivot Table

We can have our summary in the form of percentages or other relative measures. The option allows us to see the breakup of data in terms of relative measure rather than absolute value.

In the following paragraphs we will see how we can use this option to get a different type of summary. As you will invoke the field value setting, you will two tabs that you can choose from:

Summarize Value by
Summarize Value as

Summarizing Data as Percentage of Grand Total

Let's take the example of having a summary that shows percentage for each Ship Mode for different Consumer Segment for all product categories. This can be done by pointing to the row total, invoking the field value menu, select "show value as" > % of Grand Total and press OK.

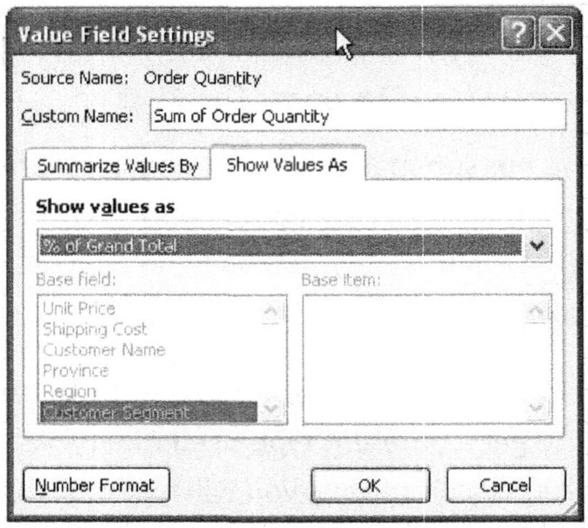

As you press ok, the pivot table will change to show value as percentages.

In this example, the value 2.66% for Consumer Segment and Delivery Trucks is calculated by dividing the Orders for this combination with the grand total of the table (to verify, switch to "Summarize by Value" mode, select option Sum and use "No Calculation Mode" to get the absolute figures. The figures when divided will give you the same results as is given by this pivot table:

5723 / 214777 = 2.66%

- We can also use relative measures to summarize the values in the pivot table besides the 11 formula provided.

2	Product Category	(All)				
3						
4	**Sum of Order Quantity**	**Column Labels**				
5	**Row Labels**	**Delivery Truck**	**Express Air**	**Regular Air**	**Grand Total**
6	Consumer	2.66%	2.20%	14.58%	19.44%
7	Corporate	4.97%	4.32%	27.26%	36.56%
8	Home Office	3.05%	2.96%	18.58%	24.59%
9	Small Business	2.71%	2.32%	14.38%	19.41%
10	**Grand Total**	**13.39%**	**11.80%**	**74.80%**	**100.00%**

SHOWING % WITH RESPECT TO COLUMN AND ROW SUM:

Referring to the Pivot Table in the last scenario, we can have breakup (in terms of percentage) of different Ship modes and consumer segments with the help of the second option in field value settings – "Show values as".

To do so, select the law row of the pivot table and select "Value Field Settings", then go the options and select "% of Column Total" and press "OK", this will show the values as percentage of column total for different consumer segments. The Grand Total for it will be 100%.

- For percentage of row total, pivot table will show the values as percentage of row total
- For percentage of column total, pivot table will show the values as percentage of column total.

In the same way you can select it to be "% of Row Total" and it will show a breakup of different ship modes for each consumer segment. In this case the row total will be 100%.

Product Category	(All)			
Sum of Order Quantity	**Column Labels**			
Row Labels	**Delivery Truck**	**Express Air**	**Regular Air**	**Grand Total**
Consumer	13.70%	11.33%	74.96%	100.00%
Corporate	13.60%	11.82%	74.58%	100.00%
Home Office	12.39%	12.02%	75.59%	100.00%
Small Business	13.94%	11.98%	74.08%	100.00%
Grand Total	**13.39%**	**11.80%**	**74.80%**	**100.00%**

Sum of Order Quantity	**Column Labels**			
Row Labels	**Delivery Truck**	**Express Air**	**Regular Air**	**Grand Total**
Consumer	19.90%	18.67%	19.48%	19.44%
Corporate	37.14%	36.60%	36.45%	36.56%
Home Office	22.75%	25.03%	24.84%	24.59%
Small Business	20.21%	19.69%	19.22%	19.41%
Grand Total	**100.00%**	**100.00%**	**100.00%**	**100.00%**

CONCLUSION:

With value field options, we can choose what summarizing figure is to be shown when we produce a Pivot Table; it could be absolute measure like, sum, count, or standard deviations or relative figure like %ages based on certain other parameter.

FEATURE # 07 CREATING CALCULATED FIELDS

Often, we are not interested in calculating simple sums or ratios from a Pivot Table. We might be looking to work out a more complex formula with several variables or any other such feature that has not been built in the pivot tables.

EXAMPLE - CALCULATING SALES – ORDER RATIO

For example we might be interested in

Sales / order to find the average size of a sales order.

Price to sales ratio

You can see from the data sheet that sales and orders are two different variables in the sheet. To calculate this ratio, there are two possible solutions:

Create a new variable and for each row to calculate this ratio. With this approach we will create and add a new variable that will be added to the actual database of the pivot table to complement our analysis.

Create a new variable within pivot table that represents the ratio of these two variable and then we add it to pivot table and perform certain analysis.

- Calculated Fields can be used to skip the manual helper columns we usually see in spreadsheets.
- They involve two or more variables (or at least one) to get calculated fields.

WORKING OUT CALCULATING FIELDS:

Option # 01

For the first one to work, we need to simply add a new column to the data and mark it as Sales/Order. The values will be calculated by taking the ratio of the two variables and you will be able to add a new variable from the actual database. But this can sometimes be really troublesome procedure if you have large number of rows (try out this procedure for some 8000+ rows of our sample data and possibly your computer will hang).

Option # 2

The second procedure is more workable – it will directly calculate a new variable and add that your pivot table. In order to do so:

Select the last row of the pivot table. This will enable the pivot table tabs and options.
Go to the tab named "Options"

Go to "Calculations" > "Field, Items and Sets" > Calculated Fields.

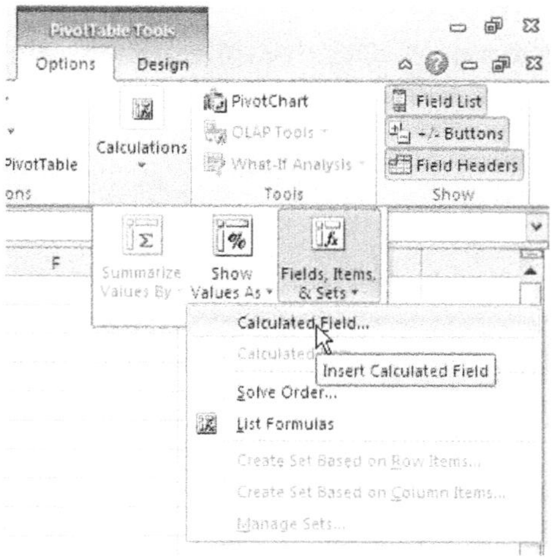

When you will select the Calculated fields, will be shown the following dialogue box:

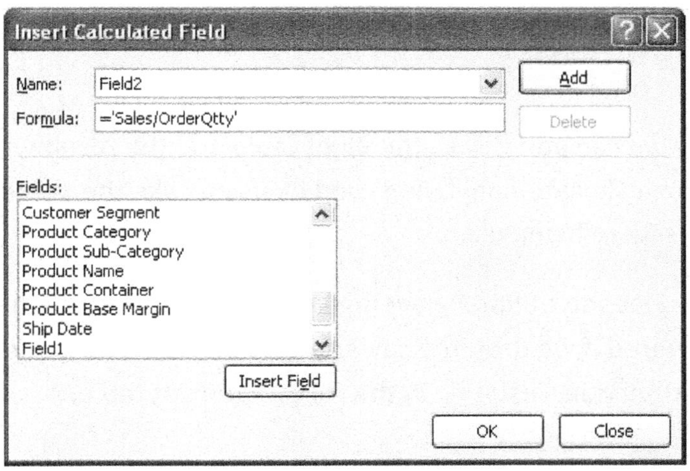

Now you can select the two fields that you want to add to this new calculated field – sales and order quantity.

Once you press OK, the formula with the name specified will be added to the fields list.

With this we will have our new calculated field.

This new field is now visible in the pivot table field lists.

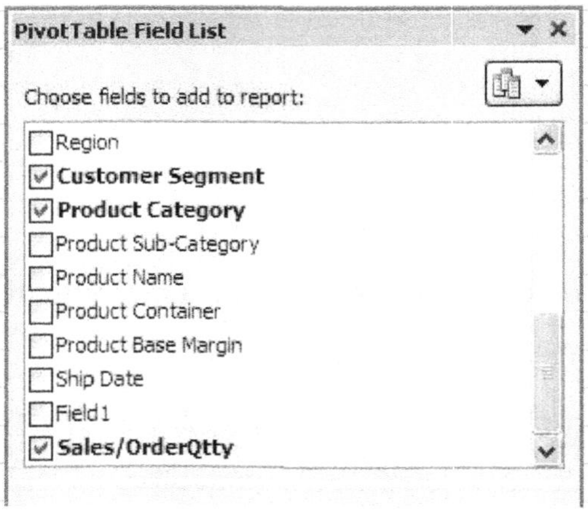

Now we can add this to the pivot table and the result will be the calculate field being used by us just like the original fields were being used.

Our question of finding average of sales per order can be answered if we drop the sales/orderquantity field to the value section, resulting in the following pivot table.

2	Product Category	(All)			
3					
4	**Average of Sales/OrderQtty**	**Column Labels**			
5	**Row Labels**	**Delivery Truck**	**Express Air**	**Regular Air**	**Grand Total**
6	Consumer	225.67	46.11	49.64	73.36
7	Corporate	223.15	47.36	45.70	70.03
8	Home Office	209.40	51.10	46.85	67.51
9	Small Business	202.81	40.52	45.55	66.88
10	**Grand Total**	**216.41**	**46.72**	**46.72**	**69.45**

EXAMPLE – CALCULATING PRICE SALES RATIO:

Let's take up the second question and see how we can solve it using calculated fields. The second question requires use of two fields again:

Price
Sales

It is actually a ratio Price divided by sales so we again go the calculated field dialogue box and setup a formula for it.

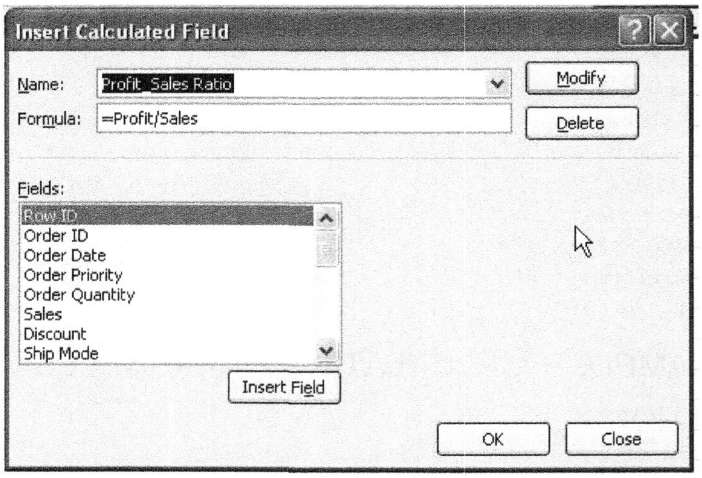

The resulting pivot table will give you the ratio for each combination of Ship mode and customer segment.

Product Category	(All)			
Sum of Profit_Sales Ratio	**Column Labels**			
Row Labels	**Delivery Truck**	**Express Air**	**Regular Air**	**Grand Total**
Consumer	0.04	0.12	0.13	0.09
Corporate	0.05	0.15	0.16	0.11
Home Office	0.02	0.10	0.14	0.09
Small Business	0.06	0.11	0.16	0.11
Grand Total	**0.04**	**0.12**	**0.15**	**0.10**

- The formulas used in creating calculated fields can be listed by gong to Pivot Table Tab > Options > Fields, Items and Sets > List formulas.

If you want to list all the formulas that are used for calculating these fields, simply click the options "List formulas", just below the "calculated field" options, you will have all the formulas for calculated fields.

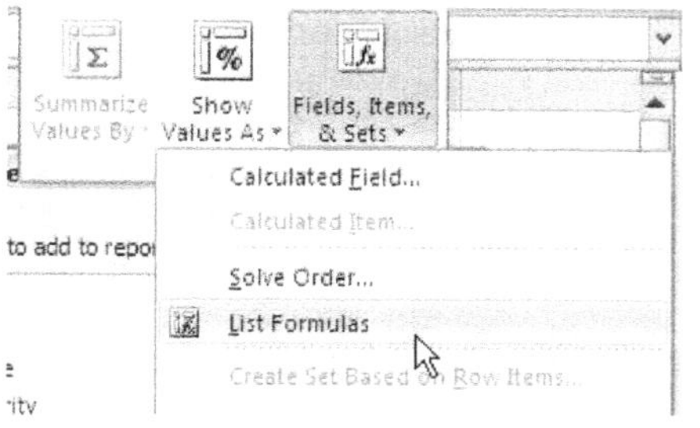

CONCLUSION:

The calculated field option is handy when you want to calculate customs fields without setting up new variable in the original database. This keeps your original database as it was and theresulting fields perform faster for larger database then manually calculated fields.

FEATURE # 08 CREATING CALCULATED ITEMS

Calculated items are another option that is available with pivot tables besides calculated fields. These two differ from each other in the aspect that calculated fields usually refer to fields (calculated or already present) whereas calculated items can work with the items available within a field.

Thus for example, the field that are available and the respective items present our table can be listed as:

Field	Item
Order Priority	Critical, Low, Medium, High, Not Specified
Ship Mode	Delivery Truck, Express Air, Regular Air
Product Category	Furniture, Office Supply, Technology

....and so on.

An example of calculated item could be to have sum of all the order that have Order Priority other than "Not Specified". Let's give this calculated item the name "Specified" that can be calculated as:

Specified = Critical + Low + Medium + High

IMPLEMENTING THE CALCULATED ITEM:

In order to implement this example, we have to add the calculated item to the pivot table. But first it will be helpful if we have pivot table without such an item and then we created a pivot in parallel with it.

- Fields contains Items – and just like fields they can be calculated by manipulating Items.

First create the Pivot table without calculated item:

Add "Ship Mode" to Row Label
Add "Order Priority" to the Row Label too just below "Ship Mode"

Add “Shipping Cost” to the Value field

The resulting table should look like table in the following picture.

Now we will calculate the “Calculated Item”:

Insert a Pivot Table selecting the New Data Table on Order_2.

a. Add “Ship Mode” to Column Label
b. Add “Order Priority” to the Row Label too just below “Ship Mode”
c. Add “Shipping Cost” to the Value field

- Beware of your computer memory or hardware when creating calculated items, their use is restricted by the hardware configuration of your computer

- You can get an error message if the computer operation to be out of its capacity.

The table should look like following picture:

	A	B	C	D	E
1					
2	**Sum of Sales**	**Column Labels**			
3	**Row Labels**	**Delivery Truck**	**Express Air**	**Regular Air**	**Grand Total**
4	Critical	390769.412	46005.2425	319973.5635	756748.218
5	High	331440.77	68150.185	394546.8575	794137.8125
6	Low	372025.902	58039.15	358491.493	788556.545
7	Medium	201133.854	60787.03	333138.7115	595059.5955
8	Not Specified	225647.278	67872.153	353519.508	647038.939
9	**Grand Total**	**1521017.216**	**300853.7605**	**1759670.134**	**3581541.11**

Now select the cell A4 ("Critical")
Go to "Pivot Table Tools" Tab > Options > Fields, Items and Sets> Calculated Items the following dialogue box will be displayed.

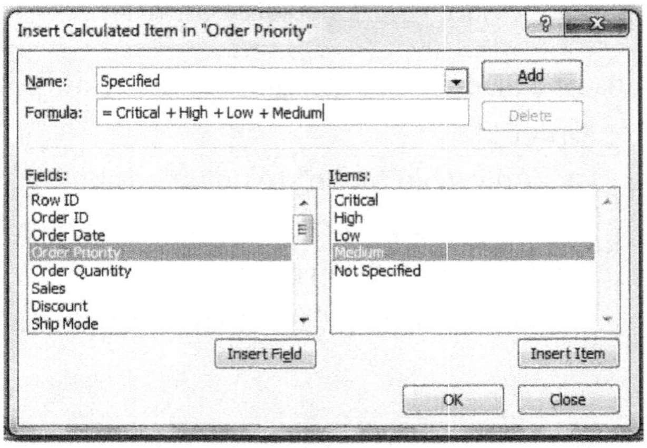

Now select the Order Priority, the Items will be shown. Keep adding one by one to the formula space until you have the entire formula as described before.
Name it "Specified".
Press Ok.

Your pivot table should have a new item named "Specified":

2	Sum of Sales	Column Labels			
3	Row Labels	Delivery Truck	Express Air	Regular Air	Grand Total
4	Critical	390769.412	46005.2425	319973.5635	756748.218
5	High	331440.77	68150.185	394546.8575	794137.8125
6	Low	372025.902	58039.15	358491.493	788556.545
7	Medium	201133.854	60787.03	333138.7115	595059.5955
8	Not Specified	225647.278	67872.153	353519.508	647038.939
9	Specified	1295369.938	232981.6075	1406150.626	2934502.171
10	**Grand Total**	**2816387.154**	**533835.368**	**3165820.759**	**6516043.281**

This new field has replaced the four previous field – Critical, Low, Medium and High so select the dropdown for Row Labels and unselect all but Specified and Not Specified. The result is the following Pivot Table:

2	Sum of Sales	Column Labels			
3	Row Labels	Delivery Truck	Express Air	Regular Air	Grand Total
4	Not Specified	225,647.28	67,872.15	353,519.51	647,038.94
5	Specified	1,295,369.94	232,981.61	1,406,150.63	2,934,502.17
6	**Grand Total**	**1,521,017.22**	**300,853.76**	**1,759,670.13**	**3,581,541.11**

You can make it a little more sophisticated by adding Ship Mode to Row Labels as well:

2	Row Labels	Sum of Sales
3	**Delivery Truck**	
4	Not Specified	225647.278
5	Specified	1295369.938
6	**Express Air**	
7	Not Specified	67872.153
8	Specified	232981.6075
9	**Regular Air**	
10	Not Specified	353519.508
11	Specified	1406150.626
12	**Grand Total**	**3581541.11**

ADDING CALCULATED ITEM TO BOTH ROW AND COLUMN LABELS:

We can add calculated items to both row and the column labels. In order to do we need to define similar criteria that we did for row labels. Let's consider a situation where we are interested in distribution of Profit over Order Priority and Regions.

Here we will define a calculated item by combining few regions and will name it as "Non-Atlantic" regions, the formula will be:

Non-Atlantic = Nunavut+ Northwest Territories + Ontario + Prarie

In order to insert this calculated item, first go to "Pivot Table Tools" Tab > Options > Fields, Items and Sets> Calculated Items the following dialogue box will be displayed.

Add the specific fields as we have mentioned in the formula and press "OK":

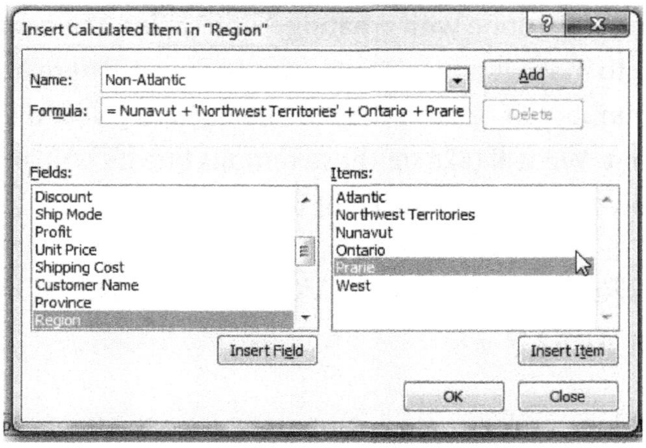

The result will be the following Pivot Table shown in the...

Sum of Profit	Column Labels			
Row Labels	Atlantic	West	Non-Atlantic	Grand Total
Not Specified	20,410.39	15,230.39	31,279.13	66,919.91
Specified	50,655.71	56,109.88	181,448.76	288,214.35
Grand Total	**71,066.10**	**71,340.26**	**212,727.89**	**355,134.26**

When the replicating fields are removed from the column labels, the result will be shown as above pivot table.

CONCLUSION:

With calculated item we can combine or manipulate the items within a field and thus can improve understanding of the data. This feature of Pivot Table makes it more flexible to work with and give results that are more meaningful. We can be more meaning full.

FEATURE # 09 CUSTOMIZING PIVOT TABLE APPEARANCES

When we are done with creating Pivot Tables, the next step is to make it appear in the way we want. There are quite number of options that can be used to give it a look we want. We will take up these options one by one and see how they change the pivot table.

WHERE ARE THESE PIVOT TABLE OPTIONS AVAILABLE?

When done with creating pivot table, click the Pivot Table Area, this will enable the pivot table options tab, click options sub tab, and on the left side you will find the following options that will invoke the pivot table options dialogue box:

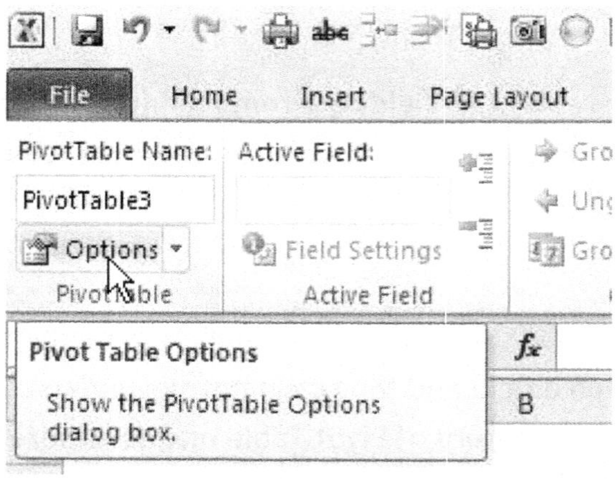

When clicked the following dialogue box will appear.

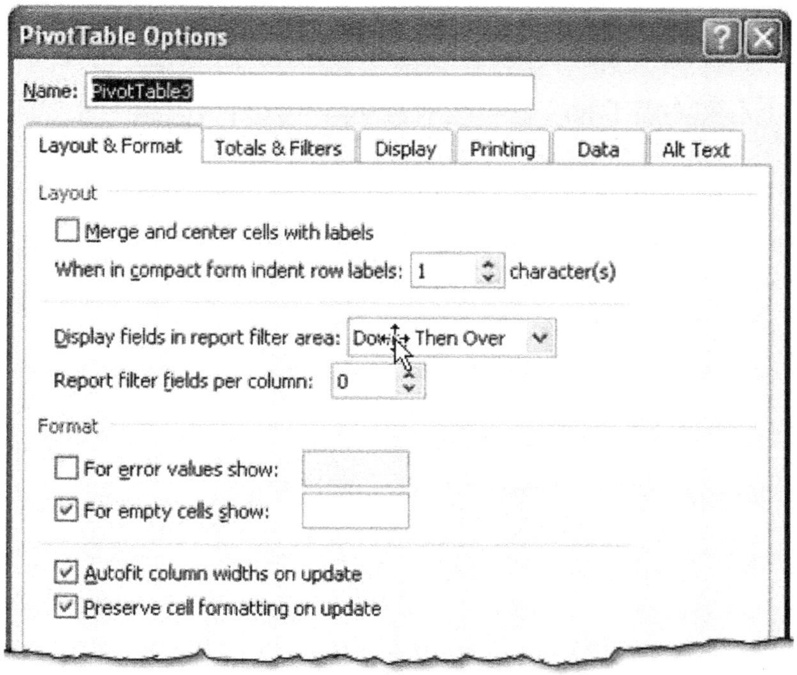

- You can control if the total row or column should appear in the pivot table or not.

LAYOUT FORMAT:

The most useful options here are following four:

Format for error values shown
Format for blank values shown
Auto fit column width on update

Preserve cell formatting on update

FORMATTING ERRORS IN PIVOT TABLES:

The error may be present in the original database and it may be result of a *calculated field* or *calculated item.* In either case, if you want to control how it should appear in a pivot table, this is the options you should use for the purpose.

You can use some custom text to show that there is an error present in the pivot table.
For numerical values, you can replace the error with zero to nullify its effect.

For example in the following case, we have encountered a division error while taking the ratio of items "count" and "frequency":

Sample Table		
Article	Count	Frequency
B	12	22
C	20	29
D	15	32
E	21	0
B	32	34
C	15	25
D	23	10

Row Labels	Sum of Count	Sum of Frequency	Sum of Count/Frequency
B	44	56	0.785714286
C	35	54	0.648148148
D	38	42	0.904761905
E	21	0	#DIV/0!
Grand Total	**138**	**152**	**0.907894737**

This division by zero error can be controlled if we format how to display the error. For example we want to display text message "DivErr" instead, the result will look like.

Row Labels	Sum of Count	Sum of Frequency	Sum of Count/Frequency
B	44	56	0.785714286
C	35	54	0.648148148
D	38	42	0.904761905
E	21	0	DivErr
Grand Total	**138**	**152**	**0.907894737**

It should be noted that in either case (formatting or not formatting error) the final result of the *calculatedfield* will remain unaffected as it is calculated as the ratio of Sum of Count over Sum of Frequency. (138 / 152 = 0.9078).

HANDLING BLANK SPACES IN PIVOT TABLES:

A pivot table can have blank spaces, depending on if there are some in the original data. These spaces might appear odd in your pivot table and you will need them to be covered anyways.

In the following table, the third entry in the field "Count" is blank and that results in a blank space in the pivot table. The solution is to use the options to cover such blank cells in Pivot Table Option dialogue box. Simply put in the space provided what you want to see in such blank cells.

- You can control how an error or a blank cell should behave (displayed or not be displayed) in a pivot table.

Sample Table

Article	Category	Count	Frequency
NPB	HPK	32	155
KGR	QIF	53	148
CPL	EHR		171
GRO	CBJ	28	108
NGO	HPK	32	160
TUB	QIF	49	163
MPK	EHR	49	192
DDH	CBJ	26	148
BJR	HPK	29	161
NRA	QIF	31	144
ASL	EHR	51	135
ORN	CBJ	39	171
BNM	QIF	37	118
JRQ	EHR	40	193
ENA	CBJ	54	119

Row Labels	Sum of Count	Sum of Frequency
⊟EHR	**140**	**691**
ASL	51	135
CPL	--	171
JRQ	40	193
MPK	49	192
⊟QIF	**170**	**573**
BNM	37	118
KGR	53	148
NRA	31	144
TUB	49	163
Grand Total	**310**	**1264**

In the above example, we have put double dashes that can be seen in the pivot table.

SHOWING AND HIDING GRAND TOTALS:

You can set if the grand total for rows and columns are to be shown or not from here. A pivot table without row and column total will look like this:

Row Labels	Sum of Count	Sum of Frequency
⊟ EHR	**140**	**691**
ASL	51	135
CPL	--	171
JRQ	40	193
MPK	49	192
⊟ QIF	**170**	**573**
BNM	37	118
KGR	53	148
NRA	31	144
TUB	49	163

CONCLUSION:

With pivot options, you can control the appearance of pivot tables very much, you can decided whether totals should be displayed at all or not, or if you want errors to be displayed as they are or should be hidden the table.

FEATURE # 10 DISPLAYING DATA WITH PIVOT CHARTS

Charts are visual way of displaying and summarizing data. Once we have created the pivot table, one might be interested in Charts that are produced on the basis of pivot table. These charts are called Pivot Carts and used Pivot Table as their source of information.

We will take up and example and see how we can create and use pivot table to display information.

CREATING PIVOT CHART:

Go to the "Insert" Tab.

Go to the "Pivot Chart", this will invoke the Pivot Chart Dialogue Box.

Select the data and point the range where you want output.

Press "ok" and you are done

- Pivot Charts provides great functionality of drilling down the data directly from charts that can not be reached with conventional charts!

The process will insert a pivot chart as well as well as a pivot table! Now one drag field to desired destination to create the chart and pivot table at the same time.

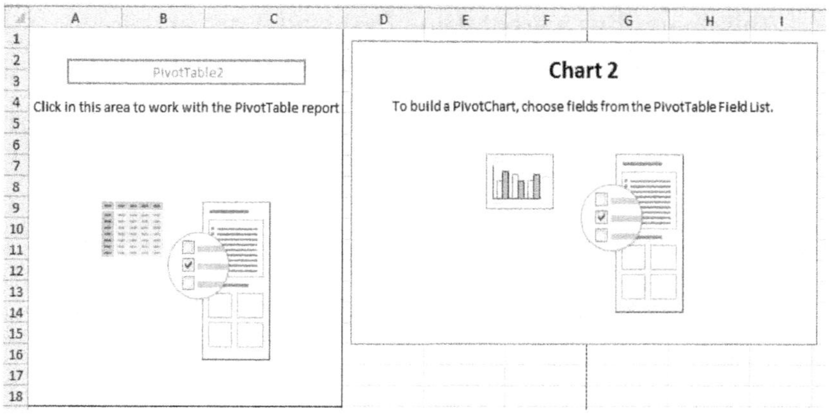

In order to add fields to the chart, let's take a scenario where we want to see the breakup of profit over various regions. In this case we will be using two fields from the database:

Sales
Regions

Dropping "Sales" to the value field and "Regions" to Row labels will result in the pivot chart as shown in the following picture:

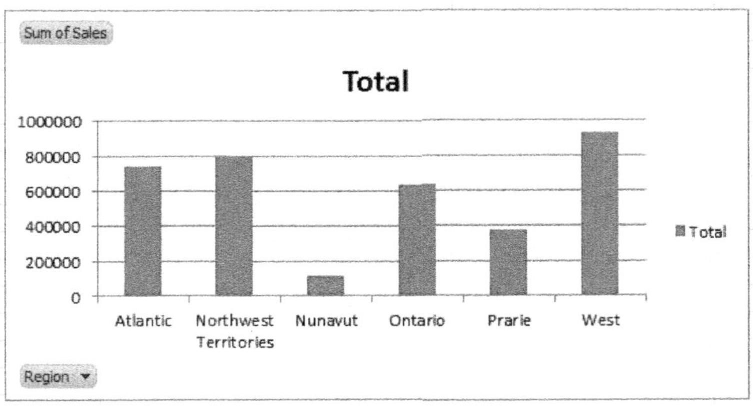

This chart adds a great value to the analysis, and is accompanied by a similar pivot table:

Row Labels	Sum of Profit
Atlantic	71,066.10
Northwest Territories	100,653.05
Nunavut	2,841.12
Ontario	95,228.74
Prarie	14,004.98
West	71,340.26
Grand Total	**355,134.26**

The above chart can be:

Can be fine-tuned to show label in the bars
formatted for color and space between the bars
Can have a different chart type as well.

CONCLUSION:

A simple Pivot Chart can be set in less then a minute if your data is ready and know what you want to plot. Pivot Charts gives you control over what has to be displayed in a chart – that is difficult when you are using conventional chart.

FEATURE # 11 CREATING MORE COMPLEX PIVOT CHARTS

The chart that we created in last section was a pretty basic chart and we can obviously create more complex ones. Since Pivot Table data is not always that simple, assuming that the corresponding Pivot Charts will be as simple as we worked out in previous parts is unrealistic. Let's see how we can add more and more data to the pivot chart.

ADDING MULTIPLE FIELDS TO VALUE FIELD:

In the following example we have created a chart that has multiple fields in the value field, show two different fields side by side – i.e. Sales and Profit.

We can continue adding variables as per our requirement but few rules of thumb can be followed for aesthetic appeal and professional look.

- Don't clutter too much information in a single chart; try to make it simple yet professional.
- Consider differences in different quantities – if they are too large, either plots them on different chart or use secondary axis within a single chart.

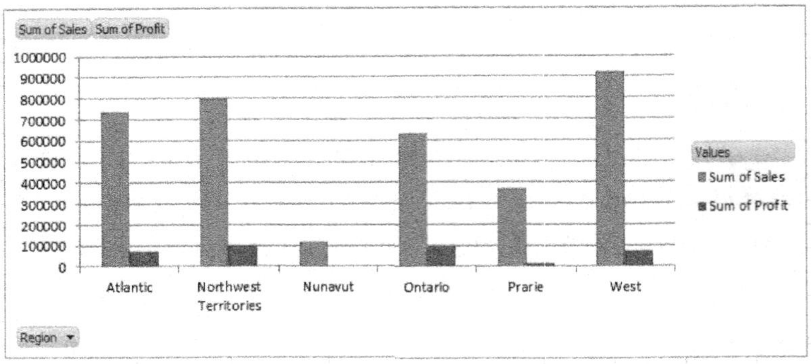

ADDING MULTIPLE FIELDS TO ROW TITLES:

We can add multiple fields to the row labels; this will group the secondary variable under various items in the primary variable. Pivot table settings are as under:

> Primary Variable is Region that is first added to row field
> Secondary variable is Transportation mode that is added next to the row field.

In the following example, primary variable plotted on the x-axis is "Regions" that are further divided in to Delivery modes and the data is thus plotted.

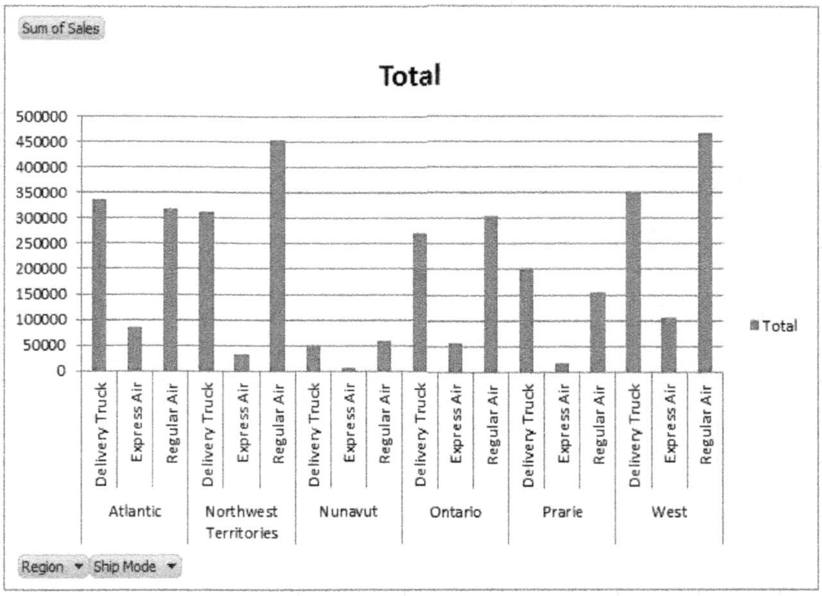

ADDING DATA TO COLUMN LABELS TO CREATE PIVOT CHARTS:

The similar chart to the one that we produced in the last example can be produced by adding shipment mode to the column field. The result is *much* easier to apprehend and has greater visual appeal.

The chart thus produced is *compactor* as compared to its counterpart that we produced earlier.

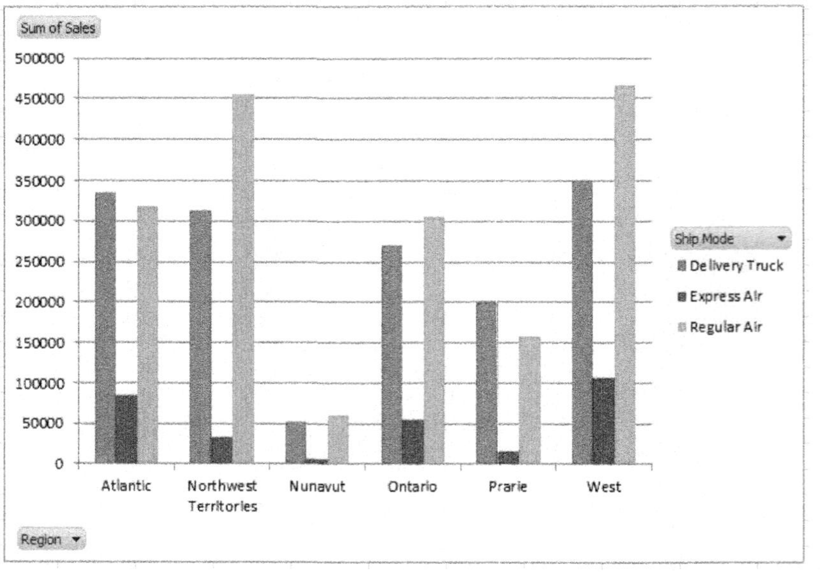
Sum of Sales
500000
450000
400000
350000
300000
250000
200000
150000
100000
50000
0
Atlantic
Northwest Territories
Nunavut
Ontario
Prarie
West
Ship Mode
Delivery Truck
Express Air
Regular Air
Region

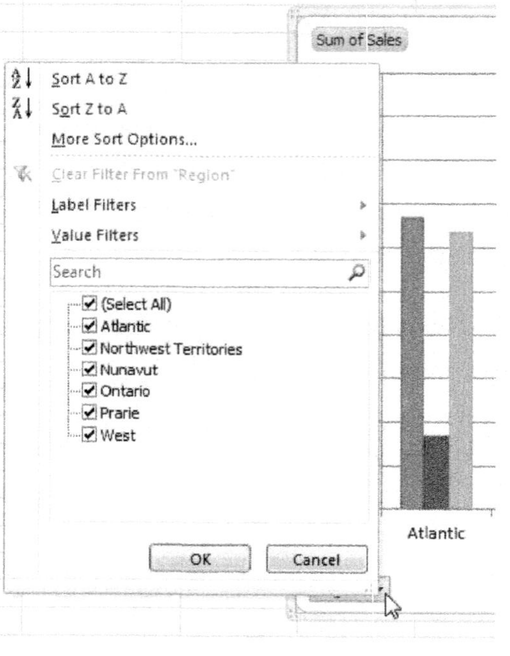
Sum of Sales
Sort A to Z
Sort Z to A
More Sort Options...
Clear Filter From "Region"
Label Filters
Value Filters
Search
(Select All)
Atlantic
Northwest Territories
Nunavut
Ontario
Prarie
West
OK
Cancel
Atlantic

FILTERING OPTIONS AVAILABLE WITH PIVOT:

The pivot charts have option to filter the data. Through this feature you can control what should be displayed on the chart. The gray drop down in the above chart will display all the items present in a field and we can select from them as per our requirement.

CONCLUSION:

There are quite number of options available that can be utilized to control what to plot through a chart. You can adjust variables as your requirement and through filters you can control if any of the item need not to be displayed.

FEATURE # 12 CHANGING CHART TYPES

Excel has variety of charts and pivot charts provide us option to select out of spectrum of charts too. It is not illogical to select chart according to the need of situation. In this section, we will discuss what variety of charts we can use with and what

Let's take up the Pivot Chart that we plotted in the last section for showing how sales is distributed over different regions and different shipment mode, we have the following chart:

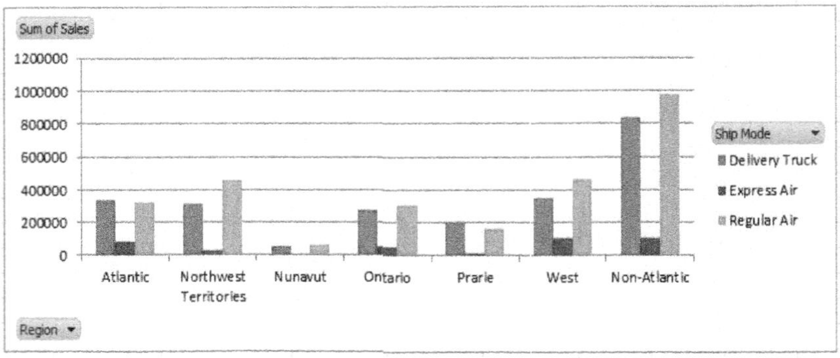

We can convert this chart into a line chart that can be used to show continuous trend of the shipment modes. In order to change the type of chart:

- Select the chart.
- Right click and select "Change chart type"
- Select "Line Type Chart with Markers" the fourth option in the series.

- Press OK

Done, the following will be displayed as the result:

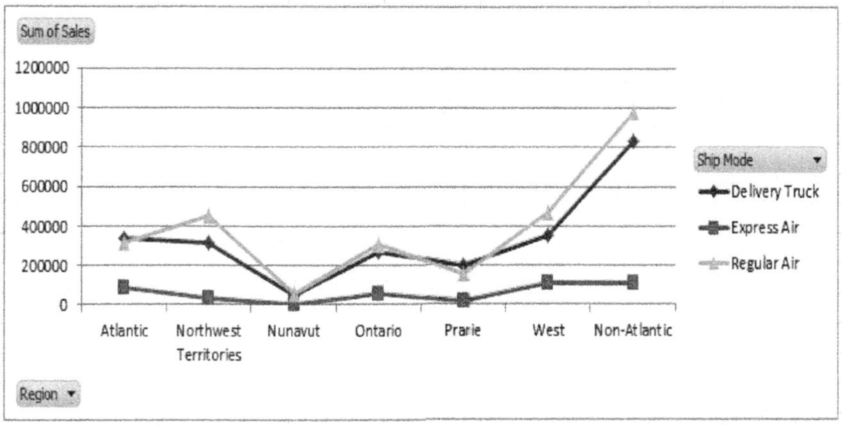

The chart provides continuous trends for the different regions and for the different shipping modes. You can play with the aesthetics of the chart and set various options.

> - Vertical gridlines are to be avoided – they make reading charts difficult.
> - Horizontal lines can be kept, but will lighter tones only – this is because we read from axis with the help of these lines.

Options Available with Chart:

The following options are the ones that are most commonly used:

Removing the grid lines – vertical and horizontal
Keeping gridlines and formatting them differently
Formatting the line to be smoothed
Formatting the line for color and markers

Let's take all these options and see how the chart changes:

REMOVING AND ADDING GRID LINES:

As a general rule, the vertical lines in charts and table are to be avoided. This is because they only distract people while reading for both charts and tables and removing them gives it a more professional look.

In order to remove lines – simply select them and press delete (be it horizontal or vertical)

Adding gridlines:

You can add gridlines by following these steps:

Select the chart first,
Go to Pivot Chart Tools > Gridlines – you will be displayed two options horizontal and vertical gridlines
Select the appropriate options
Done, lines will be displayed on the chart.

Formatting gridlines for colors etc.:

Select the gridline.
Right click, you will be shown option "Formatting Gridline"
Select this options and you can set:

- Line color
- Line Style – width or thickness, type of line, types of end line can have etc.
- Shadow and glow and soft edges

Formatting Graph line With Smooth Line, Color, and Line Variation:

You may want to change the non-smooth line with a smooth one, in order to do so:

Select the line.
Right click and select format data series.
Go to tab Line Style and Check mark smooth line.
For color, select the Color Tab and then select the color you want.

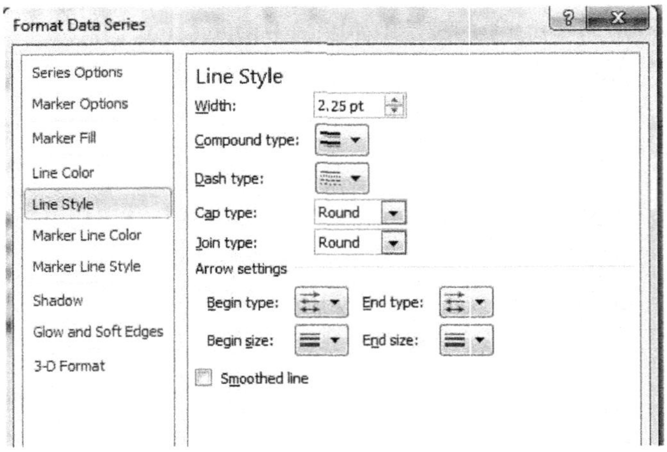

CONCLUSION:

There are ample options available to change the appearance of charts. We can tweak the gridlines, line, or bars of the charts – their color, appearance etc.

FEATURE # 13 CIRCULAR AND DOUGHNUT PIVOT CHART

Field value setting in pivot table allows us to show values and percentages of various measures. This feature can be combined to show the percentage over a total of 360 degree of a doughnut or a pie chart. Though the absolute values can also be plotted using these charts it is better to go for percentages because they are easy to understand.

EXAMPLE OF A DOUGHNUT CHART:

Let's consider the following example where are interested in showing Sales figures as absolute values over Region. The corresponding pivot table and the chart are as under.

Row Labels	Sum of Sales
Atlantic	738219.5465
Northwest Territories	800847.3295
Nunavut	116376.4835
Ontario	631132.0835
Prarie	371296.7665
West	923668.9005
Non-Atlantic	1919652.663
Grand Total	**5501193.773**

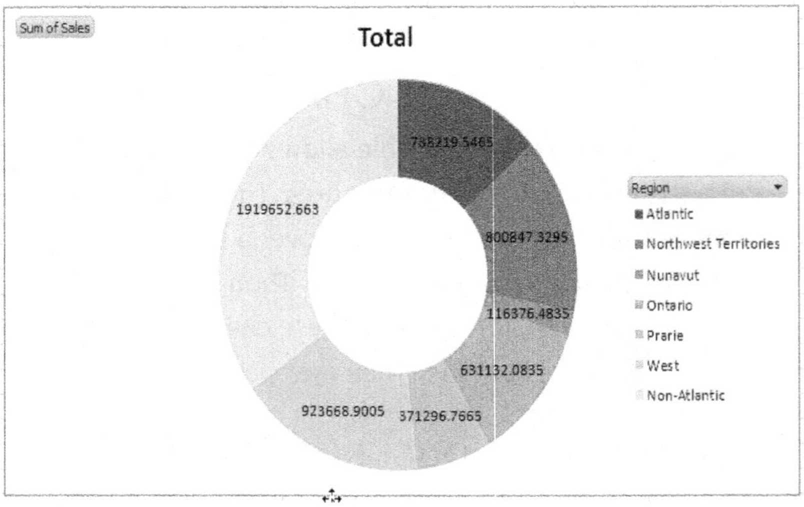

The regions in the chart can be filtered using the "Region" drop down. The sections of the chart will adjust automatically as you will select the different regions. This chart can be modified for two of their properties.

The color or theme of the chart
The numerical values for the decimal places.

The color or the theme of the chart can be adopted according to the requirement or the taste of the user. The color schemes for the chart can be accessed when you have selected the chart – through Design Tab and then selecting various themes offered therein.

- A doughnut or pie chart can work with either absolute values or percentages.

FORMATTING DATA LABELS:

Another feature of the chart that has been modified is the number of decimal places for the data labels placed on the charts. This can be done using the format data label option. Once you are done with placing the data labels:

Select the data label.
Right click, select format data label, this will display the format label dialogue box.
Select the second option "Number"
Select yet another sub-option number, which will show you different number format.
Just make sure that decimal places are set to the requirement – for our case it has been set to 02 to show only to digits after decimals.

AN EXAMPLE OF PIE CHART WITH PIVOT CHARTS

We can produce a more complicated chart within pivot chart. This time we are plotting three variables using a pie chart. The variables we are using are:

Sales in the field value place
Ship mode
Regions

Summarizing sales value for different ship modes and regions produces following pivot chart and table:

Sum of Sales	Column Labels			
Row Labels	Delivery Truck	Express Air	Regular Air	Grand Total
Atlantic	6.10%	1.53%	5.79%	13.42%
Northwest Territories	5.69%	0.61%	8.26%	14.56%
Nunavut	0.94%	0.10%	1.07%	2.12%
Ontario	4.92%	1.00%	5.55%	11.47%
Prarie	3.62%	0.28%	2.85%	6.75%
West	6.37%	1.94%	8.48%	16.79%
Non-Atlantic	15.18%	1.99%	17.72%	34.90%
Grand Total	**42.83%**	**7.46%**	**49.71%**	**100.00%**

The values in the above pivot table are modified using pivot field value option of showing individual entries as percentage of grand total, thus giving everything in terms of percentages. (This can be verified as both the column and row total stands 100%).

We can still change the way percentage are showing using different criteria's, perhaps by showing values with respect to row or column total.

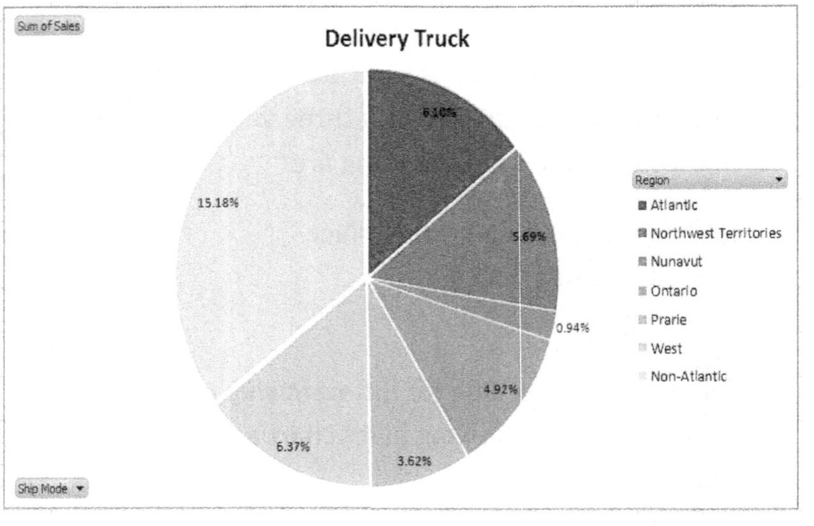

The above pie chart shows values as percentages – for all the different regions selected. We can filter the chart for different regions that will show only desired regions.

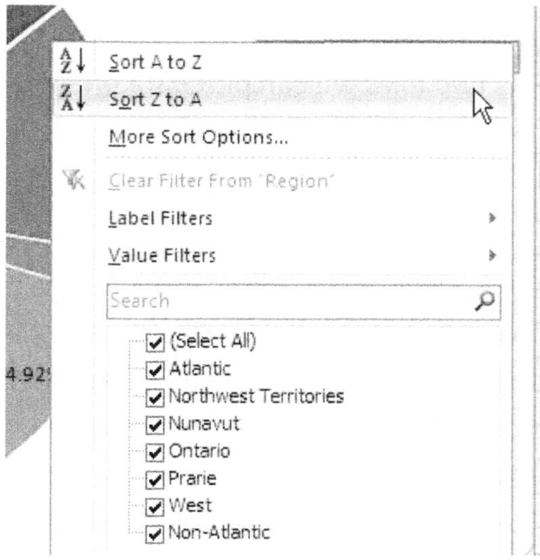

CONCLUSION:

With field value setting and using doughnut and pie charts we can show either absolute value or the percentage of the total. Percentage is easier to understand and analyze. We can format the charts for different themes as well, as per our requirement.

FEATURE # 14 PRODUCING COMBINATION CHARTS

Combination charts are charts produced with two different types of charts. Usually and at maximum two – because there are only two axes we can plot data on – primary and secondary axis.

Commonly, we found following combination of charts in reports due to variety of reasons. For example

- We want to differentiate between two variables.
- Since two variables have values that are markedly different, plotting them on one scale will make chart difficult to read.
- We just want to add some creativity to the chart.
- We are running short of space and want to accommodate more and more information to a chart.

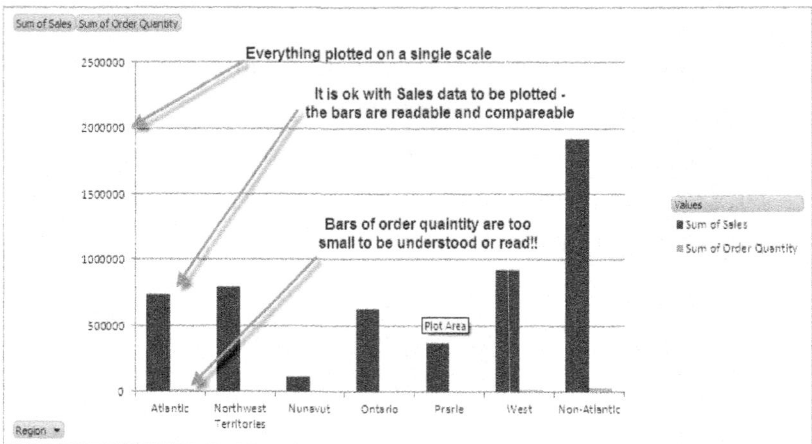

The above chart explains very well why we need a combination chart. In above chart the bars of sales are very well readable, but that of quantity are very difficult to read. Since there is a single scale, we can't do anything to improve its appearance. Here we revert to combination chart and plot the second series on the secondary axis.

- You can't not workout scatter plots, bubble charts and Stock charts when using pivot table as your data source.

HOW TO MAKE A COMBINATION CHART

Produce the basic chart first

Based on the provided order_2 insert a pivot chart.

Drag Sales and Order Quantity to value field

Move Region to row field

Once you have produced the chart (the one that looks like above);

Select the second series i.e. Order Quantity

Right click and select 'Change Series Chart Type"

This will open a dialogue box where you can select the type of chart you want to use. (There is a restriction on what chart of type you can use)

Once you have selected the chart, the series will be formatted differently on the chart.

Once done with changing the format of second series, plot it on secondary axis.

Keep series selected for further formatting

Right click and the first option will be shown will be "Series Options"

On the bottom you will see option to plot on secondary axis

Select the option

The series will be plotted on the secondary axis.

The final output will look like:

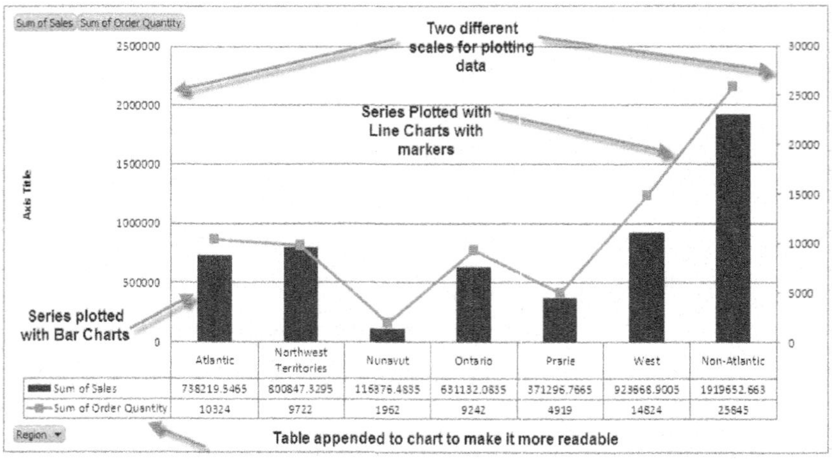

We have also added the bottom table to make chart easier to read. You can see the different scales on which series are plotted and how easy it is to read the chart.

CONCLUSION:

We can use pivot charts with more than one type of chart to display information effectively, though we cannot use all types of charts but still the functionality is great for day to day use. We have a handful options to format the chart as well.

FEATURE # 15 USING SLICERS WITH PIVOT TABLE

"Slice and dice" is a term that is used by data analysis when you manipulate data. From slice they mean taking a smaller part of a big data *or* extracting a part of a larger data set based on some criteria. From dice they mean taking another prospect of data or looking data from another angle.

Based on these definitions, we have the tool called "Slicers". This was not present in Excel 2007 and in Excel 2010 and in later version of excel, the tool come as part of the standard installation.

INSERTING A SLICER

First, insert a pivot table.
Then go to Pivot Table Tab, Options, Slicers, Insert Slicers
As you will click, a dialogue box with all available field listed will be displayed.
Select the ones that you want to add.

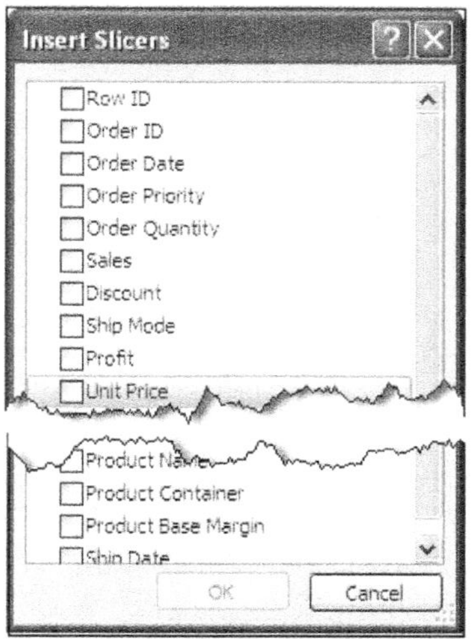

..And the slicer will be displayed it he sheet. The following picture shows how they can be adjusted for their apparent dimensions. I.e. width and height.

If the list of items in a slicer is large and we have small space available where it has to sit, the slicer will automatically have a scroll bar. Similarly you can adjust the width of the slicer to adjust for the varying length of item – text.

Individual slicers can also be adjusted for the color – different slicers can have different colors so if you want to group them in different categories it is quite easy to do.

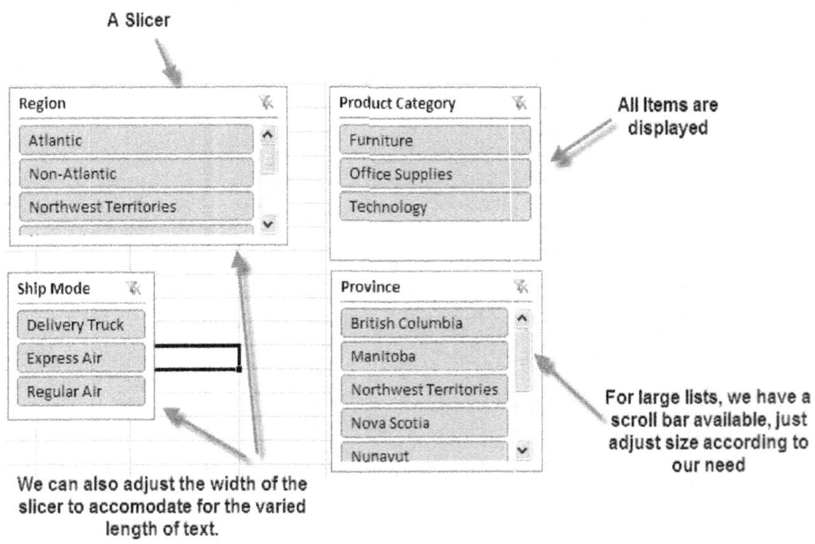

USING SLICERS TO FILTER THE DATA:

Once you are done with inserting slicers, simply select the items you want to be displayed from each – the respective changes will appear in the pivot table. In the following picture, options for regions and field are selected and corresponding result is displayed in the pivot table.

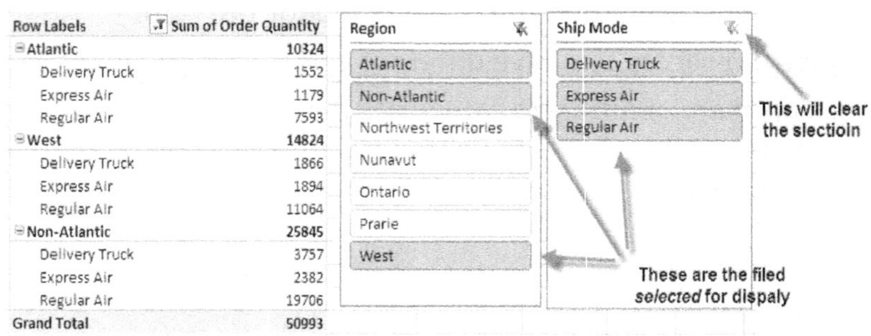

You can see that Northwest Territories, Nunavut, Ontario and Prairie are not displayed – thus if you have crated calculated items, their display can be controlled with these slicers.

OTHER SLICER OPTIONS:

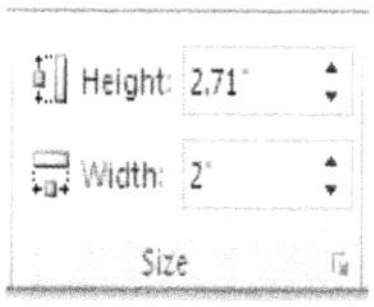

Controlling height and width of slicers – you can manually adjust the feature or enter a value in against the options. If you click the small arrow on the bottom right side, you will be displayed a whole bunch of options for formatting slicers.

More options available to format slicer

Size

Controlling aspect ratio: you can control the ratio between the height and width of the box – if you change one, the other will be changed automatically.
Column – you can adjust the number of column to be displayed in slicer – by default this value is one but the number can be increased from here.

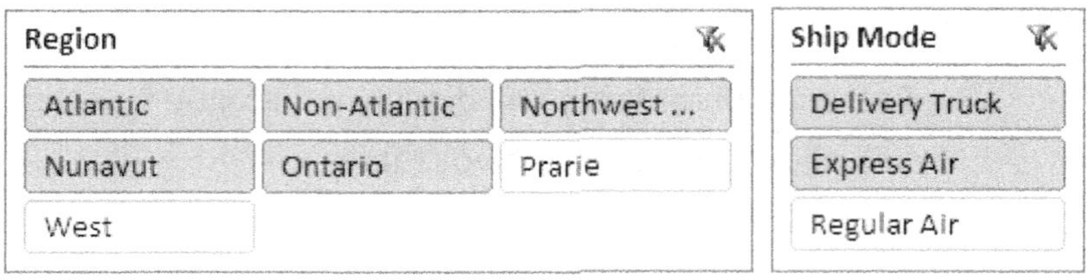

Page Layout and Position

Horizontal and Vertical position – will change where the slicer is appearing. If you check mark disable and resize option, the slicer will not change size and will be immovable.

Button height and width options – will change the dimensions of button within slicer.

Properties

You can set slicer to behave in three ways:

Move and size with cell.

Move but don't size with cells.

Don't move or size with cell.

CONNECTING SLICER TO A SPECIFIC PIVOT TABLE

Our example sheet have only pivot table and a slicer attached to it. But, we can choose the pivot table tow which we want to connect the pivot table to. In such a case that you want to change the pivot table, you can do it by:

Select the slicer, this will enable slicer setting Tab
On this tab, select "Pivot Table Connection"
Selecting pivot table will display a dialogue box that will allow selection of pivot table.
Select the one required. Done!

Example of Creating Pivot Table Based dashboard

A Dashboard is used to display meaningful and important information in a small area – be it an A4 size paper or a computer screen. Since we have discussed various aspects of creating and modifying pivot table, it's time to take our knowledge base to the next level – i.e. to create a dashboard that works on a pivot table!

Indeed will be creating two different dashboards:

First one that works "directly" on Pivot Table.
Second one that uses a Pivot Chart to display information.

Dashboard based on Pivot Table:

When creating dashboard, the first thing you need is to plan! If you don't plan, the dashboard will appear messed up and it is difficult to identify what is the exact purpose of it and how to use it get meaningful insights into data.

Purpose:

"The purpose of our dashboard is to show *how the customers' orders across different regions. The purpose of the analysis is to find how critical are the orders to them and through what means the orders are shipped from our side."*

Variables required:

The related variables or field required for this dashboard are:

Order Quantity
Regions
Product Category
Order Priority

A tentative layout of the dashboard could be like:

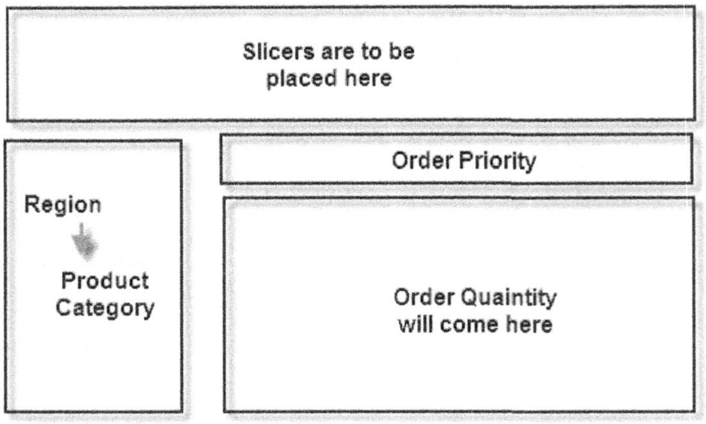

As we are done with the layout of the pivot table, we can proceed with creation of actual pivot table.

Go to Insert>Pivot Table, Select Sheet "Order (2)" – will insert the Pivot table and drag fields to respective positions (Region and Product Category in Row Labels, Order Quantity in value field and Order Priority in Column label)
Within the Pivot Table Tab, select Insert slicers, and tick mark all the four field that we want in our dashboard.

Done, we have our basic dashboard with us!

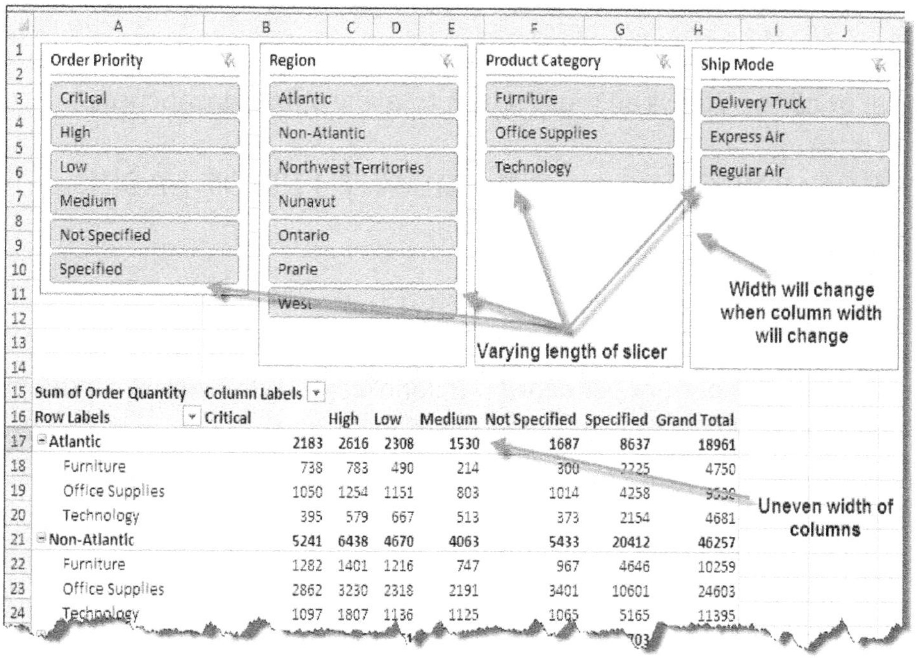

PROBLEMS WITH THIS BASIC DASHBOARD:

Though we have a basic dashboard, there are some problems with it.

The slicer layout is not in order – it does not give a look of dashboard, basically due to varying lengths of slicers. Different slicers have different number of items hence varying lengths.

If we try to make slicers of equal length, a scroll bar is added to the lengthy ones where as those with lesser items have no scroll bars – making them look a little different.

The width of fields in pivot table is not equal. This again not looks good from a dashboard perspective. Ideally a dashboard should have symmetry within to look professional.

And if we try to adjust the column widths, the slicers width also changes, we need to address this issue too.

So we need to address all these issues to make a final dashboard.

OVERCOMING THE PROBLEMS WITH PIVOT BASED DASHBOARD

Changing the length of slicers:

Since the layout of our dashboard is in landscape style, we can reduce the length of slicer by adding more columns, instead of a single column. We have already discussed how to control the number of column in a slicer – simply:

> Select slicer [Region]
> Right click, go to Slicer Tab, and set column value to 3.
> Similarly select slicer [Order Priority] and set column value to 2.

Adjust the width so that button texts are readable (not hidden) done! This will change the Slicer to the following:

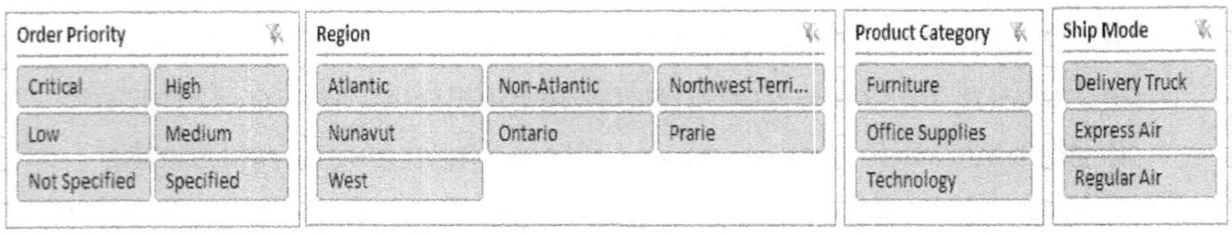

This is certainly more symmetrical and have better appearance then the default appearance.

- A very useful excel function to extract data from Pivot Table is GETPIVOTDATA(). With this function, you can use the field and respective items name to retrieve the value from the pivot table
- For example the following formula will retrieve result for Order Quantity for given field and item combination – the

result is 34.

=GETPIVOTDATA("Order Quantity",B8,"Product Category","Furniture","Region","Atlantic","Ship Mode","Express Air","Order Priority","High")

Changing the way slicers behave when column width changes.

In order to make the width of the slicers unchanged when we change the column width, we need to modify the Properties of slicers. In order to change the properties

Select the slicer and right click select "size and properties" or slicers tab and small arrow on bottom right to show the dialogue box.
Select Properties and select "don't move or resize with cells".

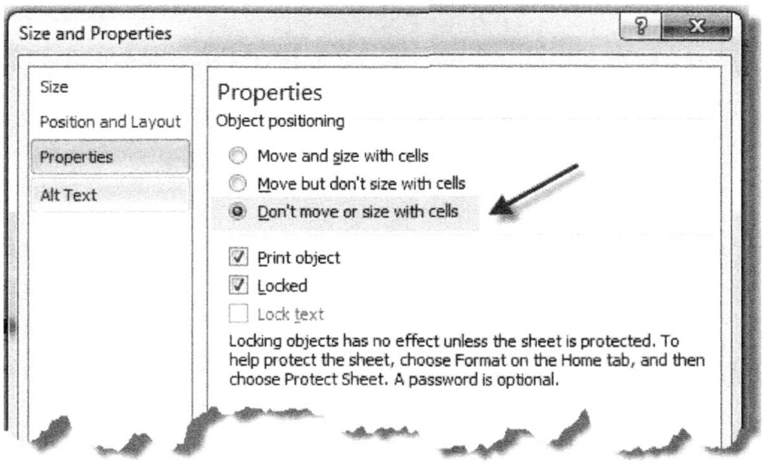

Now the slicers will not move and resize as you change the column width.

Changing the pivot table to constant column width when it refreshes:

To make the column width of pivot table fixed.

Select the pivot table
Right click, select "Pivot Table Options"
In layout and Format Tab, uncheck "Autofit column width on updates"

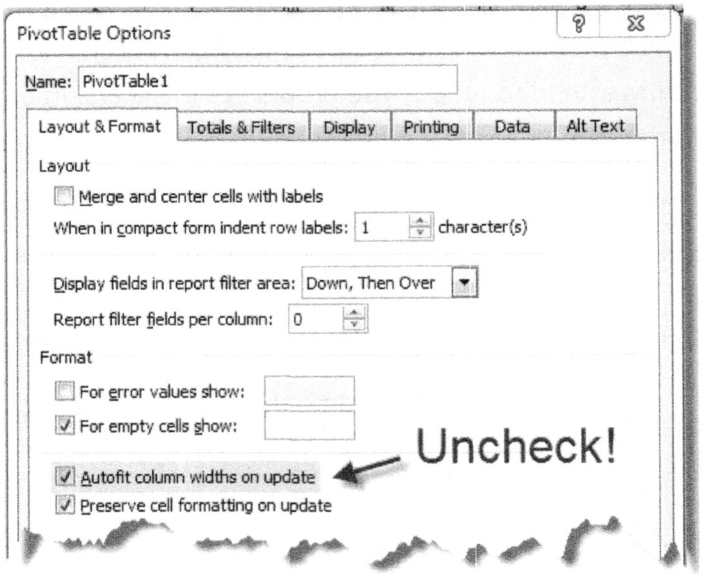

Done, the width of pivot table will remain fixed even when you refresh data.

THE FINAL OUTPUT

The final dashboard will look like:

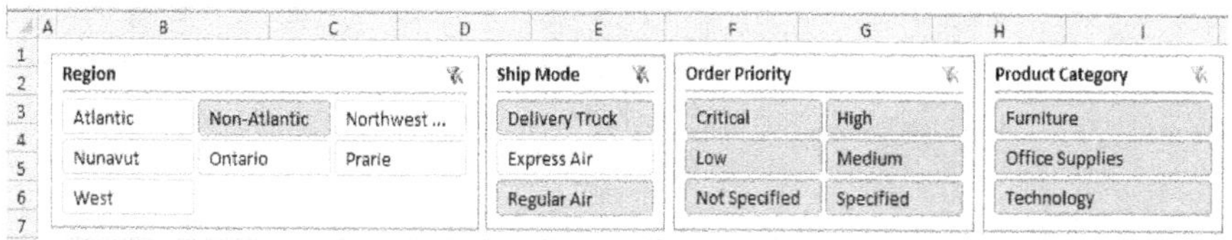

Sum of Order Quantity	Column Label						
Row Labels	Critical	High	Low	Medium	Not Specified	Specified	Grand Total
Furniture	1233	1318	1123	638	904	4312	9528
Non-Atlantic	1233	1318	1123	638	904	4312	9528
Delivery Truck	724	577	533	273	490	2107	4704
Regular Air	509	741	590	365	414	2205	4824
Office Supplies	2625	3034	1931	1948	3027	9538	22103
Non-Atlantic	2625	3034	1931	1948	3027	9538	22103
Delivery Truck	32	80	107	48	142	267	676
Regular Air	2593	2954	1824	1900	2885	9271	21427
Technology	1039	1551	1043	1064	985	4697	10379
Non-Atlantic	1039	1551	1043	1064	985	4697	10379
Delivery Truck	185	252	137	13	164	587	1338
Regular Air	854	1299	906	1051	821	4110	9041
Grand Total	4897	5903	4097	3650	4916	18547	42010

This dashboard has a good symmetrical look, the column or slicer's width doesn't change and this is our first pivot table based dashboard.

DASHBOARD BASED ON PIVOT CHART

We will be creating a pivot chart based on the same pivot table. In order to proceed we need to insert a Pivot chart, that will insert automatically a pivot table first and an accompanying pivot chart. In order to transform this into a dashboard:

> Move the pivot table well below in the sheet – at least 30 rows below, this is to give space for the slicers to be placed and the chart just below it.

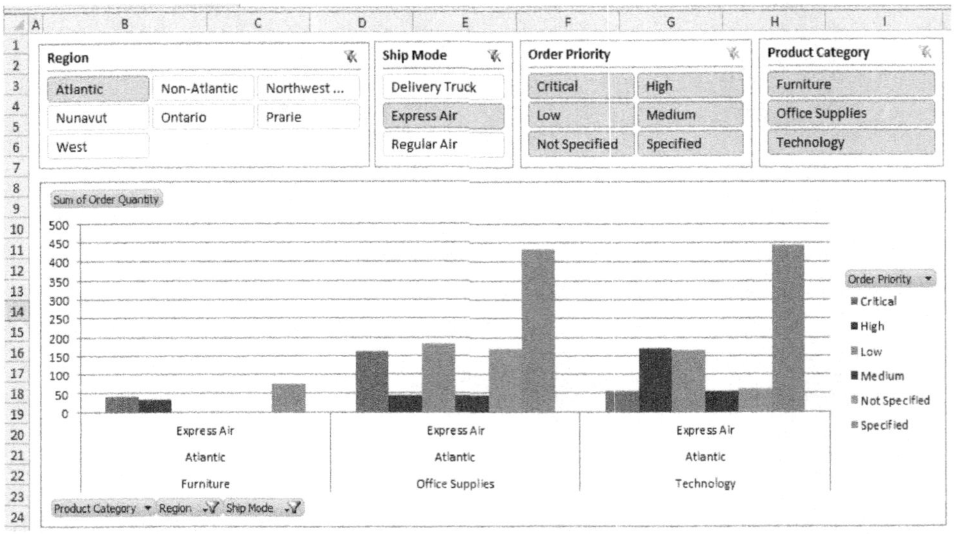

Once done, insert slicers for the variables related:

Rearrange them to give a symmetrical look.

Edit slicers for number of columns and slicer width

Add fields to pivot table – that will reflect on the pivot chart.

The above chart will be produced.

You can see that the slicer area is the same as was for the pivot table base dashboard; the pivot table accompanying the pivot chart is well below the pivot chart so that it does not disturb the dashboard.

CONCLUSION:

This is all about dash-boarding with pivot tables and charts. You can combine the pivot table and chart to produce the duo and format it the way you want.

Andrei Besedin © 2017

CPSIA information can be obtained
at www.ICGtesting.com
Printed in the USA
BVOW08s1722220418
513937BV00007B/354/P